NORTH STAFFORDSHIRE WAGONS

BY

G. F. CHADWICK

George Chadwick

12/93

WILD SWAN PUBLICATIONS LTD.

Plate 1. The opportunity to see comparative views of railway goods yards is really quite rare, and it is fortunate that two postcard views of Uttoxeter yard have survived, taken from almost the same viewpoint at least ten years apart. Uttoxeter, on the Stoke–Derby/Burton line, was the junction with the Churnet Valley route; it was also effectively the junction for the GNR's Stafford and Uttoxeter line (the actual junction being at Bramshall), and the NSR Ashbourne branch (the junction being at Rocester, on the Churnet line). Thus there were immediate possibilities of traffic from the MR via Derby or Burton, from the GNR via Stafford or Derby, and, as always, from the LNWR; the GWR, GCR, and the LYR also had connections or running powers with the NSR. The viewpoint of this (and the following) picture is between Pinfold Crossing and Bridge Street, Uttoxeter. The foreground is occupied by a GCR milk and fruit van, with two (probably NSR) low-sided wagons adjoining. The third track has a solitary GNR ventilated van, possibly No.14257. The fourth siding has four open wagons: GWR 3-plank with a load which seems to be concrete pipes; NER 6-plank No.35755; GNR 4-plank; and a 5-plank bearing the first initial G (GW or GC?). Behind, on the fifth line, are: unidentified 6-plank open: ditto, with timber load; L&Y single plank; GNR 4-plank with a load of sand; NE 6-plank. On the next line is a bogie van (possibly GNR, for milk traffic?), and the end of an LNWR 6-wheel van with corridor connection. Beyond the loading bank is a long wheelbase NSR rail wagon, then a loaded version of the same (with rails or timber), followed by a roofless NSR cattle wagon. This latter vehicle is very interesting; the design seems identical to the roofed Longbottom cattle vans circa 1900, except for the lack of a roof. Either it is a roofless predecessor of the roofed cattle vans, or it has had its roof removed and is now in use for ale cask traffic, or as a tunnel or bridge inspection vehicle (?) – the former is suspected: a post-1895, pre-1904 roofless cattle wagon? It is adjacent to a long flat truck. The next siding has four 'Ruabon' coal wagons, Nos.54, 31, 270 (?) and 298, preceded by a mysterious low van or high-sided wagon (behind the NSR cattle wagon). Further to the left, by the shunter's cabin, is an NSR 3-plank open with the single lever brake, then an LNWR flat wagon, followed by two Midland vans with an X on the doors; then a GW wagon with sheet rail (carrying casks), a GER butter van, an unidentified van, a CLC van with roof opening, and the end of an LYR van. Other wagons on view are a GN 4-plank, MR 4-plank, two GW 4 or 5-plank opens, another MR open, and LNWR van (No. 5416 ?). The Mackenzie and Holland signal at the left is interesting in having a lower gallery, and what looks like a lamp (but no subsidiary arm can be seen). A lattice jib crane can be seen under the 'Horse-Rakes' sign. This view suggests more varied traffic origins and destinations than the following photograph and perhaps total traffic has increased; the difference in foreign wagons could be accidental.

V. R. Anderson

INTRODUCTION

WHEN the North Staffordshire Railway opened in 1849, it adopted an unusual policy. Although the company possessed the necessary means to run the railway (except the experience of doing so) it did not, in fact, work the line itself; instead, it invited tenders for running the business for a period of ten years[1]. The successful tenderer was Joseph Wright, 'an extensive coachbuilder of Saltley, Birmingham', as he was later described, and 'a man of ample means, having been for many years one of the most extensive mail contractors of England'[2]. Wright contracted for the maintenance of the rolling stock and the working of the traffic, 'rolling stock' being carefully defined to include 'all the locomotive engines, tenders, passenger carriages, horse boxes, carriage trucks, luggage vans, goods, cattle and mineral waggons, and all other vehicles of every kind and description for the conveyance of persons, cattle, animals, goods, wares, merchandise, or other articles, matters or things, whatsoever on the Railway'. This description indicates that virtually all the basic types of rolling stock destined to be in use for the next hundred years had been evolved by 1849. Thus, the North Stafford Directors had provided the railway with engines and rolling stock which remained their property, though being used and worked by Joseph Wright on their behalf. In fact, George Parker Bidder, as Engineer for the line then under construction, had recommended early in 1847 that the Chairman and Directors should then obtain sample carriages and wagons from 'some three or four Carriage Builders of undoubted respectability', saying that at least 100 carriages and 1,000 wagons would be required[3]. This was done and, on 23rd August 1847, the Board resolved 'that the Engineer be authorised to procure Tenders for Twelve Goods Engines & report them to the next Board'. At the same meeting:

'Various Tenders for the Supply of Carriages were laid before the Board. Ordered, That the Secretary do write to the following parties for the supply of the undermentioned Carriages according to the Specification & Samples which have been approved by the Engineer:

To W. Hamer, Leicester,
10 Composite Carriages	@ £395 0s 0d	each
10 Open Third Class ditto	£170 10s 0d	"
10 Carriage Trucks	£106 15s 0d	"
50 Coal Waggons	£83 0s 0d	"
25 Cattle ditto	£98 10s 0d	"

To Joseph Wright, Birmingham
To Brown Marshall & Co., ditto
of each maker:
25 Composite Carriages,	@ £436 0s 0d	each
10 Luggage and Break Waggons	£298 0s 0d	"
20 Horse Boxes	£156 10s 0d	"
50 Goods Waggons high sides	£88 10s 0d	"
50 Goods Waggons low sides	£78 0s 0d	"
25 Cattle Waggons	£98 10s 0d	"

To Messrs. Royston & Robertson, Manchester
20 Parliamentary Third Class Carriages	@ £205 0s 0d	each
20 Open Third Class Carriages	£175 0s 0d	"
10 Carriage Trucks	£110 0s 0d	"
50 Coal Waggons	£83 0s 0d	"
50 Covered Goods Waggons	£83 14s 0d	"
25 Cattle Waggons	£91 0s 0d	"

To John Ashbury, Manchester
30 Parliamentary Third Class Carriages	@ £212 0s 0d	each
20 Open Third Class Carriages	£172 0s 0d	"
10 Carriage Trucks	£96 0s 0d	"
50 Goods Waggons high sides	£88 10s 0d	"
50 Goods Waggons low sides	£78 0s 0d	"
50 Coal Waggons	£83 0s 0d	"
20 Sheep Waggons	£104 0s 0d	"

The whole to be delivered between the 1st January & 1st August 1848'

This order was to cost a total of £113,555, and there are many entries in the minutes of the NSR Finance Committee[4] throughout 1848 and 1849 covering payments for 'carriages' delivered which, no doubt, also included the other rolling stock ordered in 1847. Adams & Co. are listed for payments for sample carriages, but this firm was not included in the 1847 orders placed by the company.

Thus, by the time Joseph Wright came to work the railway, not only were locomotives available, but the NSR had also provided itself with 60 composite carriages, 50 Parliamentary third class coaches and 50 open third class, 20 'luggage and break waggons' (presumably passenger stock at the price quoted), 30 carriage trucks, 40 horse boxes, 150 high-sided goods wagons, 150 low-sided goods wagons, 150 coal wagons, 50 covered goods wagons, 100 cattle wagons, and 20 sheep wagons.

Due to the survival of certain drawings and records, we know, or can reasonably guess, what these early North Stafford wagons were like. There are several definite attributions of NSR carriages, and some of wagons; it is also likely that several anonymous drawings refer to North Stafford wagons.

It may appear from the Board minute that George Bidder approved drawings, specifications and samples put forward by the several firms of carriage and wagon builders, rather than getting tenders for rolling stock which he had designed for the company. However, it does seem that some general specifications and drawings were used as a basis for the tenders, as not only are some of the prices identical between builders, but the Finance Committee minutes show a payment on account of £241 14s 6d to C. F. Cheffins, 'for making plans and drawings, &c. of Carriages &c.' on 11th October 1848. Cheffins was a 'Mechanical and Architectural Draughtsman', well-known for his lithographs of railway maps, and he was also a surveyor employed by the NSR for plans of new lines in 1846 and 1864[5].

The two definite NSR wagon drawings, bearing no other name, are of a coal wagon and a sheep van. These drawings are in a collection made by the Great Northern Railway circa 1848-50[6], apparently being representative of the current practice at that time. Apart from the Great Northern, a number of railways are represented in the collection, though mostly only by a single vehicle. Drawings for the East Lincolnshire, Great Western, Leeds, Dewsbury and Manchester, London and Birmingham, and London & York Railways are included in

Plate 2. This (earlier) view of Uttoxeter yard can be dated as after 1902 by the presence of the NSR low-sided wagons in the foreground, whose numbers show that they were built by the Metropolitan RC & W Co. in or after that year; there are no wagons with the large 'NS' lettering, so the date would seem to be before the introduction of that lettering style (1912). It is noteworthy, too, that Midland wagons seem to be the only 'foreign' company represented here. The wagons nearest the camera, left to right, are: NSR 2-plank wagons Nos.6164, 6286, and 6346 (?), followed by a single-plank NSR wagon, all built to Longbottom's designs. On the next line are two MR 4-plank wagons, followed by three NSR 4- or 5-plank dumb-buffered loco coal wagons whose numbers are illegible, but display a variation in the positioning of the word 'LOCO'; next is a PO coal wagon, probably belonging to Eckersley Bros. of Uttoxeter, then an MR van, an anonymous sheeted wagon, and three 4- or 5-plank opens, one of which is carrying machinery. The next line has several examples of Eckersley Bros. coal wagons, and one other PO wagon, with 'William ...ings' visible on the top plank. The sidings in the background accommodate many NSR low-sided wagons with the small lettering style, and also one cattle van (which is not NSR). There is also a mysterious haystack! The signal (at the far left, background) can be identified on both views, as can the second crane, just discernible in front of the unidentified van under the 'Horse-Rakes' sign.   *Dr. J. R. Hollick*

addition to those for the North Staffordshire. Several other drawings are also attributed to 'J. Wright, Builder, London'. It is a matter of conjecture as to whether all these drawings are originals from the various companies or builders, or whether the originals were re-drawn by GNR draughtsmen; certainly the drawings vary quite considerably in size and style, and seem to be by different hands. Even the paper differs. However, a number of drawings are apparently by the same hand on the same paper, and have the same lettering style; this includes the two definite NSR wagon drawings, and also at least four others. In addition, there are two drawings of presumed NSR non-passenger carrying coaching stock (a horse box and an open carriage truck), with four certain and one probable drawings of NSR carriages. The four additional wagon drawings comprise covered goods, high-sided goods, low-sided goods and cattle wagons. All six plans

of goods stock appear to be by the same builder or designer, the vehicles possessing identical ironwork, axle guards and boxes, couplings, side-chains, self-contained buffers, and brake gear (except for the sheep van, cattle wagon and covered wagon, which are unbraked). None of the drawings by J. Wright, Builder, is included in this batch, so presumably his firm was not the originator of these designs. John Ashbury was the only builder to supply the NSR sheep vans, so it may be that the appropriate drawing came from his firm. Royston & Robertson may have supplied the covered wagon drawing under the same circumstances, although it seems much more likely that these are Cheffins' drawings, or copies from them.

The North Staffordshire carriage drawings comprise a passenger luggage van, a Parliamentary third class carriage, and a composite carriage,[7] with an underframe relevant to all three. These are attributed to the NSR by the original GNR index, and are on similar paper and drawn in similar style to the goods stock already mentioned; there is also a drawing of an open third class carriage, which appears to be one of the same set. None of the NSR's builders at this time supplied all four types of carriage stock, so, whilst we now know what the earliest NSR carriages were like, we cannot attribute any one type to less than two or three builders. This may lend credence to the view that these GNR-collected drawings are those made by Cheffins, or copies from them. Perhaps the NSR lent a complete set of the drawings to the GNR, for all the types of vehicles (goods and passenger) originally ordered by the NSR are covered here; none is missing. Apart from these, only the drawings attributed to J. Wright have any pretension to covering a range of rolling stock types, and the latter are signed by Wright's firm, in most cases bearing his draughtsman's name – Kirkman.

The Wright drawings in this GNR set cover two varieties of high-sided goods wagon (one with an end door), a goods wagon, a coal wagon, a ballast wagon, a timber wagon, and a 'break' wagon for the London & Birmingham Railway (a most curious beast, that!). These, together with the NSR stock and the GNR's own products, give a general picture of the state-of-the-art in carriage and wagon building at that time, not dissimilar, of course, to the plates of Daniel Kinnear Clark's delightful collection[8]. The vehicles of other companies to be seen on NSR metals (especially those of its near neighbour, the LNWR) are well represented by Clark. Further, the fact that Joseph Wright's firm was to be one of the most prolific future suppliers of rolling stock to the North Stafford is also helpful in discerning the probable appearance of the 'Knotty's' trains up to at least the 1870s and '80s.

Plate 3. The NSR's 'knot' design of builder's plate (bottom left) was used on passenger and other coaching stock. The wagon plate (top left) is a later version; previously, there had been a rectangular plate bearing the letters 'NSR' with the wagon number below (cf. wagons 4748, 2221, 01113, etc. in following illustrations). The Metropolitan RC & W plate was to be found on both batches of wagons and carriages built by the North Stafford's favoured contractor, e.g. wagon 6176 of 1902, and many of the radial 6-wheel carriages and bogie stock. The Ashbury Company was a subsidiary of the Metropolitan Company.   *Author*

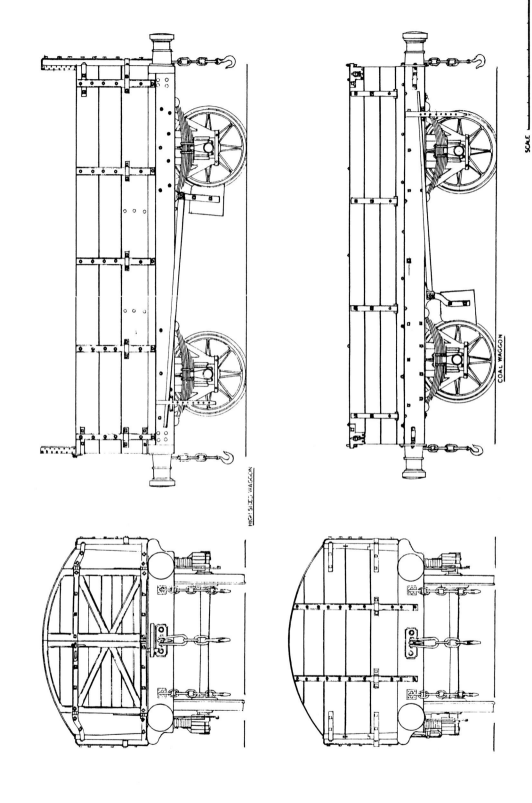

Fig. 1. Early open wagons, 1849: a high-sided, 3-plank wagon with doors at one end, and a 3-plank, dropside coal wagon (bottom right). Both these wagons have spring buffers (self-contained), a single lever brake, 4-link couplings with hook ends, and 5-link side chains.

(E. G. Mackenzie)

HIGH SIDED WAGGON

COAL WAGGON

SCALE

CHAPTER ONE

EARLY WAGON DESIGN ON THE NORTH STAFFORD

THE three open wagon types ordered by the NSR in 1848 present an interesting contrast in view of the later development of these (and other) designs. The low-sided wagon would be almost immediately recognisable on the 'Knotty' more than half a century later. On a 9ft wheelbase, with one-plank sides 13½in high, it was to be the forerunner of several thousand low-sided wagons that the railway would order. This version had self-contained buffers, grease axle boxes, the simple sledge brake, and a 3-link coupling with a hook end, as well as similar (but 6-link) safety chains. It appears that one end plank was fastened to the sides in a different manner than at the other end; the purpose of this is not clear, although it may be that this end let down to take longer loads.

The second vehicle in this group was a coal wagon, with 3-plank drop sides giving a total height of about 24in, though the opening section was about 1½in less than this. The wheelbase was very short, a little under 8ft. Ironwork and brakes were identical to those on the low-sided wagon.

The most interesting of the three wagons was the high-sided version, with an 8ft 6in wheelbase and 3-plank sides, 36in high. The sides were secured by five heavy vertical straps. However, the ends were the most interesting feature; these were rounded, and 4½ planks high (42in). One end was plain, except for two long vertical metal straps and the returns of two horizontal corner straps. The other end had two outward-opening cupboard type doors, wooden-framed and cross-braced, with two long strap hinges to each door. The running gear on this wagon was identical to that on the other two, except that the brake lever was applied from the left-hand end, not the right, as was the usual practice. There was also a footstep plate over the coupling hook at this end. This was the door end, and may have had something to do with the brake arrangement. The brakes on all three types appear to have been on one side only.

The covered vehicles comprise a van and a sheep van, together with at least one type of roofless cattle wagon. The van had an 8ft 3in wheelbase and was outside-framed, having two sets of cross-bracing frames to each side with plain double doors between, opening outwards. The ends had two vertical stanchions in addition to the outside frame members; the roof was battened. Running gear was similar to the arrangement on the open wagons except that, as was then the practice, no brakes were fitted to the vans.

The sheep van was an interesting vehicle, and although its underframe was very much like that of the covered van, it had a longer wheelbase (9ft). This van was double-decked, with two sliding doors on each side to each deck. The sides were of vertical iron rods spaced 3in apart, with wooden vertical framing only at the door openings. Ends were framed, but no vertical stanchions appear; in fact, the construction appears just a little flimsy. Again, this van was brakeless. It would be interesting to learn how the top deck was loaded!

The 1848 cattle wagon had an 8ft 6in wheelbase. Its sides were framed externally, most of their length being taken up by the doors, whilst the ends were strongly cross-braced. The top two-thirds of both sides and ends were open, and the vehicle unroofed, as would be the case with such wagons for most of the following 50 years. The ironwork included self-contained buffers, side chains, hooked coupling chains, and axle guards and boxes like the van, sheep van, and the wagons.

A second type of cattle wagon, built a little later by Joseph Wright & Sons of Saltley, Birmingham, was also a much more substantial vehicle than the sheep van – one reason, perhaps, why these cattle wagons lasted so much longer. A solidly framed vehicle, initially built on an 8ft (with later batches on an 8ft 6in) wheelbase, the cattle wagon had diagonally-braced framed and boarded sides for two-thirds of their height, with open frames above. There were double, outward opening doors above a drop flap portion as a loading way. It seems likely that the sides were solid down to floor level, i.e. no inspection or ventilation gap at floor level, as in later practice. Again, the ends were solidly framed and boarded, with diagonal struts, apex upwards – a design feature common to most recorded North Stafford vans after this time. The Wright running gear differed from the other early NSR wagons in the detail of the axle guards and boxes, in having 3-link coupling chains only, and in the buffers. These latter were self-contained 'rubber' buffers, much used by the North Stafford for at least 55 years subsequently. No brakes were fitted.

Early railway carriages and wagons showed evidence of the traditional methods of construction used in horse-drawn vehicles in their woodwork and general design. There is, though, some evidence that the woodwork of railway wagons became simpler and less elaborately constructed as the demand for rolling stock increased and, with it, the capital which had to be invested; outside frame construction for wagons, as opposed to vans, did not last too long. Likewise, some aspects of the ironwork were simplified. It is noteworthy that the wagon plates in Daniel Kinnear Clark's *Railway Machinery* of 1855 show only one such vehicle with dumb buffers (this a timber wagon), the rest being fitted with metal self-contained buffers, or even fully-sprung buffers with the springing

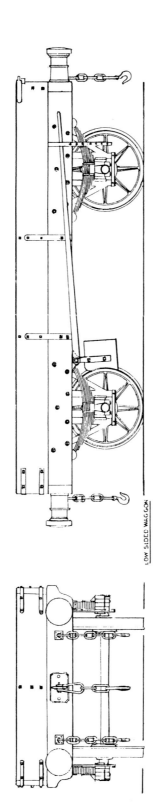

LOW SIDED WAGGON

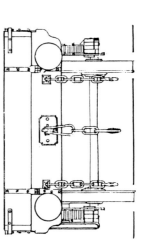

Fig. 2. Early open wagons, 1849: a low-sided, single-plank wagon which, like the 3-plank vehicles previously shown, was fitted with spring buffers, single-lever brake, 4-link couplings and 5-link side chains.

(E. G. Mackenzie)

attached to the central cross-members of the wagon frame. Clark does not discuss dumb buffers in detail in his treatise, though he does elaborate on the other types[9]:

'Buffing and Draw Springs.

'To what has already been said of the buffing and draw springs of the carrying stock, it may be added that many kinds of springs have been thus employed. India-rubber springs are much used, formed of circular discs of that substance strung upon the buffing and draw rods. Also, helical and spiral springs, formed of a rod of steel twisted into a coil or volute; of which the section has usually been circular, but is now made oval, on John Brown's system, and with advantage. The "volute" proper, as made by Spencer, is made of a plate of steel twisted into a coil, and has already been referred to. Cork and other materials have been used for buffers; but they are now set aside, and the forms and material above enumerated are those now principally in use.'

In 1855, it may have been true that sprung buffers were in use, but it is unlikely that their use on ordinary goods wagons was to continue for long. The widespread adoption of dumb buffers on such rolling stock made construction simpler (and cheaper), and was considered quite adequate at the time; a load of coal would not complain about buffering-up shocks, or even incur the broken legs of carriage occupants mentioned by Clark! Most railways required thousands, rather than hundreds, of open wagons, and the money saved by simplifying construction was very substantial. The difference can be seen from the NSR minutes. In 1849, high-sided goods wagons were costing £88 10s 0d each, low-sided were £78, and coal wagons £83, whilst in 1854 Wright was supplying coal wagons at £72, reduced to £53 each in 1862; low-sided wagons were £52 10s 0d in 1863, and new wagons in general were estimated at £66 each in 1864. Thus, savings in the order of 20% (or even 25%) could be made in ordinary wagon specification and construction.

Although contemporary graphical evidence is lacking, it does seem that by 1860, the form of goods rolling stock had crystallized on the North Stafford into a long-lasting pattern, as was the case on other railways. Low (1- or 2-plank) vehicles characterised the wagon stock in use for general merchandise, with 3-plank wagons being employed for coal traffic.

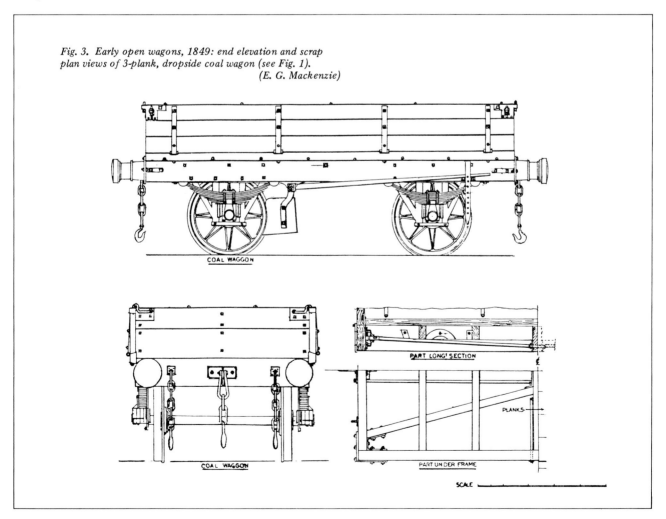

Fig. 3. Early open wagons, 1849: end elevation and scrap plan views of 3-plank, dropside coal wagon (see Fig. 1).
(E. G. Mackenzie)

Fig. 4. Sheep vans were provided in 1849. These were double-decked and looked a bit flimsy in construction, without brakes; one conjectures how the top deck was loaded.
(E. G. Mackenzie)

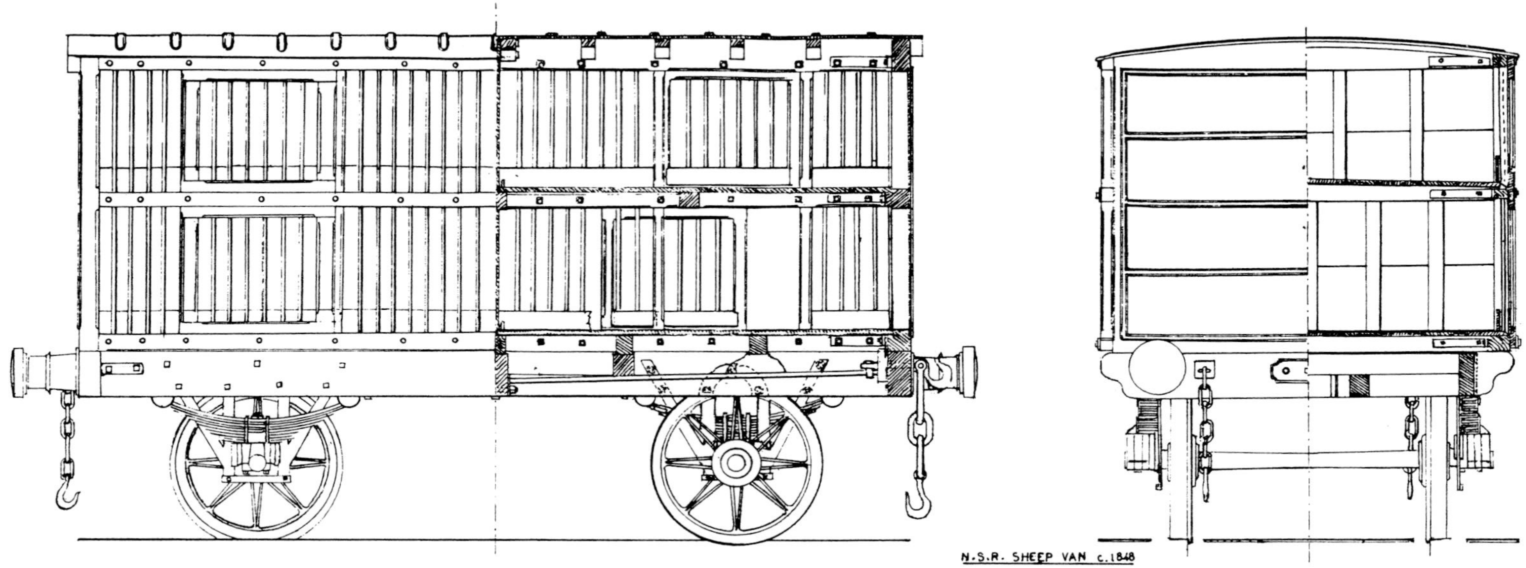

N.S.R. SHEEP VAN c.1848

N.S.R. COVERED VAN c.1848

Fig. 5. The North Stafford had relatively few goods vans. Here is one of the original 1849 batch: outside framed, as all the NSR vans were to be, side doors, unbraked, 4-link couplings with hook ends, and side chains; the buffers are self-contained.
(E. G. Mackenzie)

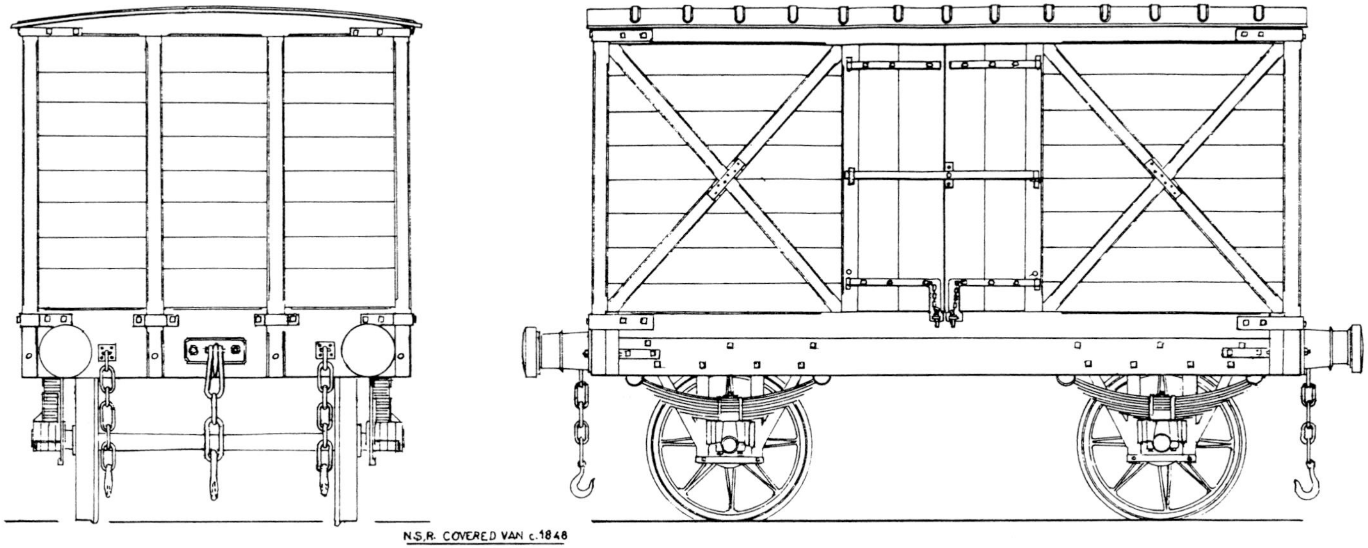

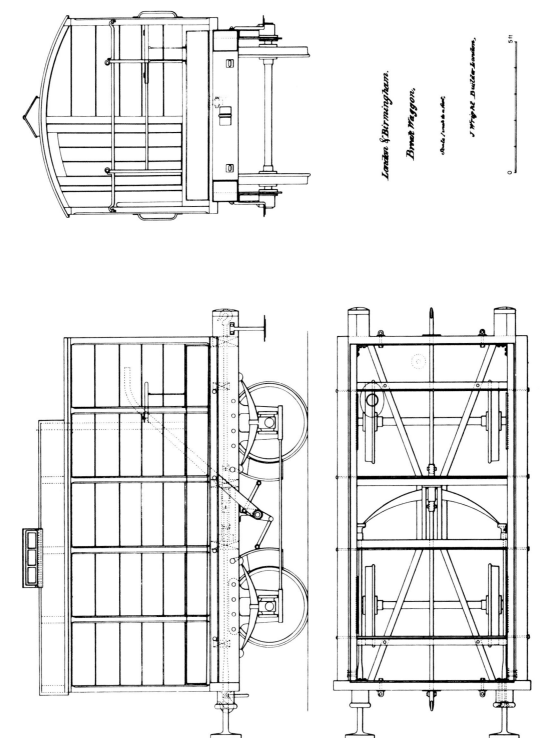

Fig. 6. It is possible that brake vans of a pattern similar to this London & Birmingham Railway vehicle, built by J. Wright & Sons, may have been supplied to the North Staffordshire Railway c.1849-50. The van is windowless, it seems, and has both dumb and spring buffer sets; the large brake lever operates on only two wheels. (HMRS)

London & Birmingham.

Break Waggon.

Scale 1 inch to 1 feet.

J. Wright Builder London.

5 ft

END ELEVATION

FRONT ELEVATION

PLAN OF SUPERSTRUCTURE

SECTIONAL PLAN

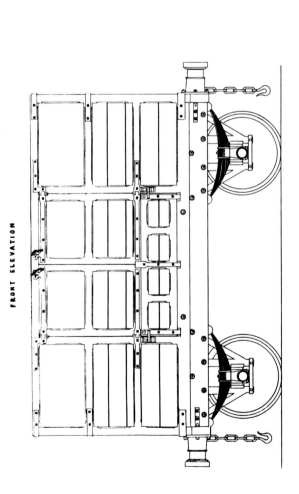

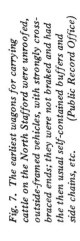

CATTLE WAGGON

Fig. 7. The earliest wagons for carrying cattle on the North Stafford were unroofed, outside-framed vehicles, with strongly cross-braced ends; they were not braked and had the then usual self-contained buffers and side chains, etc.   (Public Record Office)

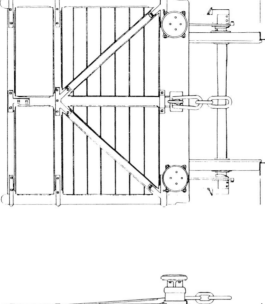

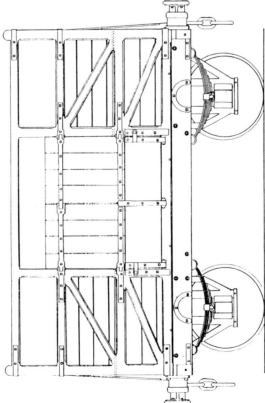

Fig. 8. A further type of cattle wagon was supplied by Joseph Wright in 1855. They were outside-framed, but of a different pattern and ironwork arrangement from the 1849 batch; importantly, they were fitted with the self-contained rubber buffers that appeared later on many reconditioned wagons, and were still to be seen in this century.

(E. G. Mackenzie)

Fig. 9. The 1848 horse box with groom's compartment; the vehicle is fitted with square-faced buffers.   (Public Record Office)

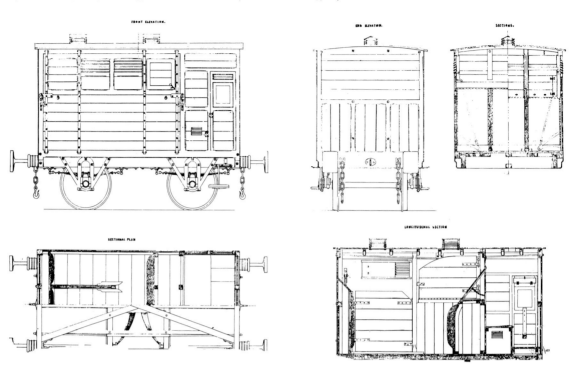

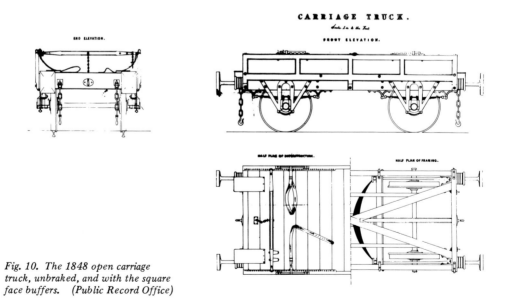

Fig. 10. The 1848 open carriage truck, unbraked, and with the square face buffers.   (Public Record Office)

CHAPTER TWO
THE FIRST CHANGES

EVEN before Wright took over responsibility for running the line, the rolling stock position was being amended. Mr. Forsyth, the Resident Engineer, reported in November 1848 that he had sold 16 ballast wagons at cost price to Messrs. Brassey & Co., contractors for part of the line, with an undertaking to repurchase them at valuation at the end of three years.

Also in November 1848, Mr. Bidder reported 'that two more Goods Break Vans were required', and it was agreed that they be procured. This is interesting as, rather curiously, no goods brakes were included in the original (1847) orders, although it appears from this minute that some had already been purchased, even as an afterthought. It is tempting to speculate that Wright may have provided the NSR with some of the London & Birmingham type, with its huge lever, but this is pure conjecture.

February 1849 saw 13 of the goods wagons being 'made fireproof' at a cost of £213 10s 0d; again, no details of the operations involved have survived.

The order for two goods brake vans was seemingly confirmed in June 1849, at which time '2 strong cranes, one for Stoke, one for Uttoxeter' were ordered, though it is not clear whether these were mobile or fixed cranes.

Wright entered upon his contract to run the railway in July 1849, at which time the stock was valued at £240,000, being composed of '981 Carriages and Engines', i.e. all kinds of rolling stock. November saw a request from Wright which was approved by the Traffic Committee: 'Engine to be purchased from Mr. Price at £1200 to be worked between Burton and Tutbury'.

North Staffordshire Railway Rolling Stock Returns

From the Report of the Engineer, G.P.Bidder, 15th July 1848:

Locomotive Engines Ordered	60
Passenger Carriages	160
Luggage Vans	20
Trucks, Coal Waggons, Cattle Waggons, Horse Boxes, and Goods Waggons	690

This is in addition to the samples made previous to contract, which amounts to 45 Waggons & Carriages.

From the Report of the Directors, January 1851:

Carriage and Waggon Stock:

Coupées	2
First Class (Composites altered)	4
Composites	59
Second Class	22
Third do.	86
Horse Boxes	36
Carriage Trucks	33
Luggage Vans	35
Covered Waggons	58
Goods, Cattle, & Mineral Waggons	759
Omnibuses	6
Vans, etc.	6

Although the North Stafford Directors (or their advisers) had no doubt estimated the probable numerical requirements for rolling stock with which to work the anticipated traffic of the line, it seems that they had underestimated the goods traffic to some extent. In consequence, 55 wagons were purchased from George Merrett, the civil engineering contractor, in June 1849 (at £56 each) and, by June 1850, 100 wagons were on hire from Wright. These 100 vehicles were subsequently purchased from Wright by the company for a total of £6,000.

The Traffic Committee minutes of this period shed a little light on the kind of traffic which was being carried on the North Staffordshire Railway, most of which persisted in various ways for the whole of the company's life.

Salt was one such traffic, the minutes for 12th January 1852 noting that: 'Mr. Leake of Whitehall Salt Works near Wheelock offered to find his own Waggons for the conveyance of salt', under certain conditions which were agreed. On 21st September 1852, 'The Application of Mr. Blackwell Salt Works Wheelock to hire from this Company 40 Salt Waggons was deferred for future consideration'. Mr. Blackwell seemingly did not get his NSR wagons for, on 11th July 1854, an accident to a goods train near Leigh was reported. It was attributed to 'the breaking of an axle of a Salt Waggon hired by a Mr. Blackwell of Wheelock Salt Works from the Manchester, Sheffield & Lincolnshire Railway'. Midland Railway wagon No. 8134 was said to have been 'broken all to pieces' in the accident.

Traffic in salt and flints was being carried between the Potteries and Gainsborough, and is thought to have continued for a long time; it seemingly arose from the canal connections of the NSR.

Ironstone traffic commenced on 11th July 1853, running from the Whitebarn Company's works at Apedale to Bloomfield station (via Norton Bridge), trains of up to 20 'trucks' being despatched every Monday, Wednesday and Friday.

Subsequently, on 23rd August 1853, the minutes read:

'Reported and approved the transfer of the following Carriages of the North Stafford Company to the use of the London & North Western Company Viz:-
10 Horse Boxes, No.1/10 – Brown Marshall & Company, Makers
10 Carriage Trucks, No.11/20 – Royston & Robertson, Makers.'

It would appear that the NSR had overestimated the need for these particular types of vehicle, although the transaction may have been one of hire, rather than sale. The stock numbering information is unfortunately too meagre to draw any worthwhile conclusions as to the initial numbering of the NSR rolling stock.

Returning to open wagons, on 2nd November 1852, it was 'Resolved that 100 Waggons be ordered to be built for the Company's use if that number cannot be hired from

Mr. Wright'. Two weeks later, it was reported that Wright had no wagons for hire, but was to supply six samples for approval at £48 each. This appears to have led to specific purchases from Wright & Son, recorded in the Finance Committee minutes, of 30 wagons in December 1852, 34 in February and 70 in March 1853, all at £48 each, indicating low-sided, dumb-buffered wagons. In April, June and August 1853, 25, 65, and 50 wagons respectively came from Wrights at £64 each, possibly high-sided vehicles. Six 'Goods Break Vans' at £130 each were also supplied by Wright in December 1853, following a delivery of an unspecified number of such vehicles in May of that year.

Meanwhile, on 29th November 1853, the Traffic Committee first deferred and then acceded to Mr. Forsyth's requisition for a further supply of wagons, comprising 100 low-sided, 50 high-sided, and 50 cattle – 'to be ordered of Mr. Wright if he will make them at the same prices as the last'. Unfortunately, the tendered response did not please the committee at its meeting on 13th December 1853:

'For each Cattle Waggon	£95
For High-sided do.	£87
For Low-sided do.	£72 and £2 10s 0d each extra for adapting a number of the last mentioned for the Carriage of Timber'.

The matter appears to have been resolved for, on 10th January 1854, Mr. Forsyth reported that he had ordered 50 low-sided wagons from Wright & Son. Also, on 7th March 1854, 'Mr. Forsyth reported that he had ordered a second supply of 50 New Waggons at £66 each without Spring Buffers which might be included at an additional cost of £8 per waggon and the same was agreed to with the addition of Spring Buffers. It was further ordered that one hundred more waggons be obtained by instalments of fifty on the same terms'.

These orders were responded to as follows: 20 waggons (at £72) were supplied by Wright in March 1854, followed by a further 30 (also at £72) plus 10 at £66, in May 1854; 40 new wagons (at £66) were also provided by Wright at the end of May. Then in August 1854, 30 new 'Coal Waggons' were supplied by Wright at £72 each, and also 20 new 'Timber Waggons', Nos. 1 to 20. These were the North Stafford's first timber wagons, and must have replaced some earlier stock carrying the same numbers, possibly the vehicles which had been 'transferred' to the LNWR. October 1854 saw 25 new 'Goods Waggons' (probably high-sided) provided by Wright, at £87 each. Then in December, a 5-ton travelling crane was supplied by S. Ellis & Co. of Salford, and Wright also supplied 25 new cattle wagons at £95 each, probably to the 1849 drawing. In 1856, 97 further wagons (at £70 each) were purchased from J. Wright & Son, plus 3 'Goods Break Vans' at £130 each.

J. Wright & Son supplied 50 new wagons (Nos. 1797 to 1846) at £68 each in March of 1857, followed by another

49 at £68 and one at £87 in April. Samuel Ellis & Co. supplied another portable crane (this one rated at 10 tons) to Alton station in August 1857, for £150.

By the end of June 1859, when Wright's contract to work the railway had expired, the North Stafford had therefore increased its rolling stock to something of the order of 2,000 goods vehicles (it was 2,286 at the end of 1860[10]); there is no means of knowing what the wastage of wagons was over the decade in which Wright had worked the line. It is clear, though, that Wright was using some of his own engines and rolling stock for various additional purposes from time to time, indicating some kind of deficiency in the NSR stock, albeit temporary. For example, Wright supplied engines for ballasting in 1858, and there are also two interesting entries in the Finance Committee minutes concerning the further supply of engine power; on 1st March 1859, 'J. Wright & Son, for Engine power Burton to Leicester Junction & back, from 1st Decr. 1856 to 31st Decr. 1858, £271 2s 6d' – and a similar entry in September 1859.

The settlement with Wright at the end of his contract for working the line involved Benjamin Fothergill 'Examining and Valuing Engines, Tools, &c.' in November 1859, as a result of which Wright's firm was paid a further £1000. However, the association with Wright did not end there, and his firm, under various names, was to continue to supply the North Stafford with rolling stock for most of its remaining years, despite the railway company eventually setting up its own locomotive, and carriage and wagon works.

Thus, on 31st January 1860, we find a payment to J. Wright & Son:

2 New pattern Mineral (Wagons) as per Account certified	£117 10s 0d
One Quarter's hire of 60 Mineral (Wagons) from 21 June to 30 Sept.	£178 8s 2d
31 Decr. £180, less repairs	£168 3s 3d
	£464 1s 5d

It would be interesting to know what the 'New pattern' wagons were like.

The North Stafford was still hiring wagons, but this time from the Midland Wagon Company (from 1860), 250 wagons being involved. The NSR continued the hire of these particular wagons until March 1865, when they were purchased at £24 each, after a valuation by John Seddon.

Meanwhile, J. Wright & Son continued to supply new vehicles, with 101 mineral wagons, Nos. 2451 – 2551, being paid for in June 1862 (at £53 each). Then, by way of a change, William A. Adams supplied 102 new wagons, Nos. 2552-2653, in August 1862; 100 of these cost £53 each, one £55 5s 0d and one £51 5s 0d. Wrights then provided 20 new timber wagons, Nos. 2654-2673, at £50 each (also in August), whilst 20 wagons were on hire at that time from John C. Harvey for a short period. By March 1863, Wright's firm had become the Metropolitan Carriage and Wagon Company, and they provided 100

Fig. 11. NSR open wagon No. 1897, showing both old and new buffing arrangements, with dumb buffers to the left, and webbed casting spring on the right. (Author)

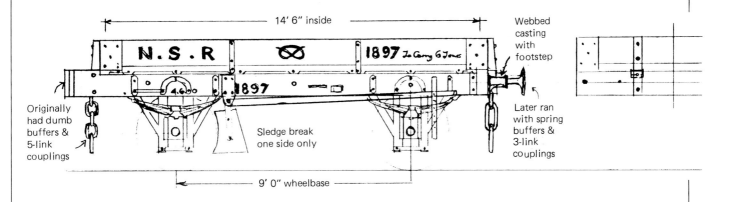

14' 6" inside

Webbed casting with footstep

N.S.R ⊗ 1897 *In Carry G Jones*

1897

Originally had dumb buffers & 5-link couplings

Sledge break one side only

Later ran with spring buffers & 3-link couplings

9' 0" wheelbase

Plate 4. Open wagon No.1897, photographed on a Leek & Manifold Valley Light Railway transporter car, presumably the only reason for the photograph. The wagon is quite elderly, probably having been built in 1857 by Joseph Wright & Sons, of Birmingham. The vehicle is likely to have followed the general dimensions for a 6-ton wagon: 14ft 6in by 7ft (internal) on a 9ft wheelbase, with 11in sides. Originally, it would have been fitted with dumb buffers, but is shown here with the webbed-stock sprung variety, flattened on top of the casting to form a footstep; these date from at least the 1870s, and are mounted on what are likely to be new headstocks. No.1897 has received new drawgear and three link couplings. The axleboxes are the early, flat-bottomed grease box type, with the central boss bearing the initials of the company. An early sledge brake, one side only, is fitted.

J. W. Walker

Fig. 12. *Open wagon No. 2949, shown with both the original dumb buffer and the subsequent reconditioned rubber (self-contained) type. Apart from the detail at the left-hand end, the drawing shows the vehicle in its 1905 condition.* (Author)

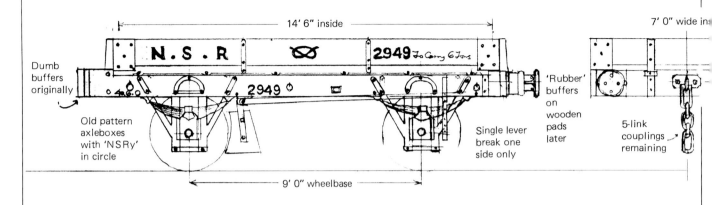

14' 6" inside

7' 0" wide in

N.S.R · ⚭ · 2949 *To Carry 6 Tons*

2949

Dumb buffers originally

Old pattern axleboxes with 'NSRy' in circle

9' 0" wheelbase

Single lever break one side only

'Rubber' buffers on wooden pads later

5-link couplings remaining

Plate 5. Wagon No.2949, portrayed aboard an L & MVLR transporter. Like No.1897 on the previous page, this wagon was built by Joseph Wright & Sons, although by the time of construction (1864) that concern had become the Metropolitan RC & W Co. Ltd. Again, the vehicle would probably have measured 14ft 6in by 7ft, with 11in sides, on a 9ft wheelbase. This photograph (1904) shows the vehicle in a later guise, although the wooden pads, rather worn on top from being used as footsteps, may represent cut-down dumb buffers; alternatively, they were specially-made pads for use as seatings for the self-contained 'rubber' units shown, which themselves were likely to have seen service on older, scrapped vehicles. No.2949 still has the original 5-link chain fitted. Nos.1897 and 2949 represent perhaps the most characteristic of North Stafford goods stock, a basic type which stemmed from the original wagons of 1848, and was later to appear as single or 2-plank 8-ton stock.

Manifold Collection

new low-sided mineral wagons at £52 10s 0d, followed by a further 100 (Nos. 2774-2873) in April; it seems likely that the March batch bore numbers 2674-2773.

On 6th October 1863, the Traffic Committee resolved to obtain tenders for a further 200 wagons, and on 1st December tenders were opened as follows:

	per sample	per sample with Blaenavon tyres
	£ s d	£ s d
A. & W. C. Shackleford, Cheltenham	66 4 0	63 10 0
Midland Waggon Co., Birmingham	66 10 0	65 10 0
Railway Foundry, Bradford	66 15 0	64 5 0
Tatley & Co., Chorley	54 0 0	60 0 0
" " " corrected by telegraph	52 0 0	56 0 0
Robert Crossland, Bradford	71 10 0	-
Metropolitan Railway Waggon & Carriage Co., Birmingham	64 12 0	63 0 0
Brown, Marshall and Co., Birmingham	not according to specification	
Gloucester Waggon Co., Gloucester	67 17 6	65 17 6
Wm. Stableford, Oldbury	67 17 6	63 18 0

The tender of the Metropolitan Company (once again) was accepted on 15th December 1863, for 200 wagons at £64 12s 0d per wagon, the whole order to be delivered within three months. At the same Committee, there was a complaint from a customer:

'Mr. Heath waited upon the Committee to complain of being short of waggons for the conduct of his traffic and he was informed that 200 waggons had already been ordered and that if necessary a further supply would be ordered & it was Resolved, looking to the early determination of the Contract for the hired Waggons, to recommend the Board to order 250 additional Waggons.'

The Metropolitan wagons duly arrived early in 1864, and the Finance Committee minutes record a payment for '100 low-sided goods waggons', Nos. 2974-3073; although not so recorded, the balance of 100 wagons in this order were presumably Nos. 2874-2973. The Traffic Committee minutes, which exist to July 1867 (when it was amalgamated with the Finance Committee) show the progress of rolling stock orders. For the same period, the Finance minutes show payments for rolling stock delivered; after that time, of course, the two were minuted together. It seems likely that some items have been omitted from the Index to these minutes, and occasionally even from the minutes themselves, though other confirmatory evidence of this is difficult to find in most cases.

In 1864, the North Stafford Finance Committee apparently took stock of the company's financial situation, for a 'Statement of Capital Account' appears in the minutes, dated 11th May 1864. The 'Summary of the Account' includes an item: 'Engines, Waggons & Vans ordered: £29,000', which is broken down under a further heading of 'Probable Expenditure on Capital for Works Proceeding' into:

6 Engines & Tenders @ £2440	£14,460
10 Goods Break Vans @ £114:	£1,140
200 New Waggons @ £66:	£13,200
(Total) Engines, Waggons & Vans Ordered:	£28,980

A further entry: 'New Works, Land & Private Waggons required: £101,000' is also broken down as follows:

Required (inter alia)
1,200 private Waggons on the line more or less say at an average Cost of £50 each:	£60,000

The idea of the NSR buying up private wagons had apparently begun very early in 1864, for the Traffic Committee minutes[11] for 13th January 1864 record:

'Resolved, that the General Manager be instructed to report upon the practicability and desirability of acquiring upon fair terms the private Waggon Stock now working upon the line'. The General Manager reported to the committee on 8th March 1864, and his report was recommended to the Board for adoption, the Board duly resolving that the recommendation be adopted on 9th March. Unfortunately, there is no inkling in any of these minutes as to the reasons for the decision; the GM's report is not quoted. However, it is stated that the wagons were to be purchased at valuation.

A Special General Meeting of the proprietors of the company was called on 11th May 1864, at which the Chairman spoke of the 'advantage and economy to the Company of acquiring the private waggons working on the Railway'. The meeting concurred in the expediency of increasing the rolling stock and enlarging the workshops and station accommodation of the company out of existing capital. It is probable that the reasons advanced by the Midland Railway, when they carried out a similar purchase of private owners' stock in 1882, applied to the North Stafford's exercise. Private owner wagons gave rise to much empty return working, and they were often poorly maintained. The NSR could, it believed, give a better, more economical service in properly maintained wagons, of which it needed more. However, the main effect may have been simply to provide the private owners concerned with money to buy themselves further lots of newer wagons.

It does not seem that the whole of the projected 1,200 wagons were purchased, although the stock of the NSR did increase by 1,232 between 31st December 1863 (when it had 2,411 wagons) and 31st December 1864 (3,643 wagons[12]); this represented a 50% net increase in one year. To judge by the prices paid, many of the wagons purchased were new, or nearly so, and it could not have been a question of buying up old or obsolete rolling stock, which might have been a nuisance for the company to handle. However, most of the vehicles that were purchased seem to have been on hire from various wagon builders. The list of wagons bought by 30th September 1864 was as follows[13]:

Bidder & Elliott	252 waggons for	£10,000
Henry Hargreaves	12	£72 17s 0d
F. Goddard & Sons	15	£881 17s 0d
White Barn Co.	71	£2,693 8s 11d
R. Heath	61	£3,484
Chatterley Mining Co.	20	£1,070
Silverdale Coal & Iron Co.	70	£3,350 8s 0d
W. Bowers	6	£312
J. C. Harvey	94	£2,233
High Carr Mining Co.	25	(no entry)
	646	

Henry Hargreaves' 12 vehicles were owned by the Birmingham Waggon Co. and it also appears that the Goddard wagons belonged to the Metropolitan RC & WC (5 wagons) and the Lancashire & Yorkshire Waggon Co. (10 wagons). The Chatterley vehicles were owned by the Midland Waggon Co., the Harvey wagons by the Birmingham Waggon Co., and the High Carr vehicles by the Warrington Waggon Co.

A further 12 wagons are recorded later in the Finance Committee minutes as being purchased from Leigh & Bradbury at £44 2s 6d each, and 20 coal wagons, the property of the Lancashire & Yorkshire Waggon Co., were bought at £67 10s 0d each from Knutton Farm. These make the total of wagons recorded as purchased from private owners in 1864 as 678. In January 1865, John Seddon was paid £126 for 'Valuing Private Waggons', presumably those listed above. A further 20 Birmingham Waggon Co. vehicles came from Harveys in March 1865, bringing the total of private wagons purchased at that time

to 698. However, the NSR brought a further 250 wagons, already being used by them and on hire from the Midland Waggon Co., in April 1865 (as already mentioned) at a total cost of £8,500.

The records of the Birmingham Railway Carriage & Wagon Co.Ltd. apparently show three transactions with the NSR about this time[14], dated November 1863, January and February 1864. The 1863 item was for 10 6-ton wagons (Nos. 130-139), on hire purchase at £3 11s 11d each year for five years; the 1864 items were for 10 wagons (Nos. 1973-1982) in January, and 12 (Nos. 2017-2028) in February. However, no orders for purchases of new wagons at these times can be traced in the NSR minutes, though there are entries relating to the purchase of wagons then on hire by private owners from the Birmingham Co. It seems conceivable, therefore, that these entries relate to such private wagons, possibly those from Henry Hargreaves and J. C. Harvey. However, there is further difficulty in the running numbers quoted, if they were NSR numbers; Nos. 130-139 must have been replacement numbers from scrapped stock, and Nos. 1973-1982 and 2017-2028 are rather out of sequence, these running numbers having been reached by the NSR in the late 1850s. Alternatively, it is possible that these Birmingham wagons were hired to the NSR in the late '50s, and finally purchased by them as part of the 1864 buying-up of private vehicles – like the purchase from the Midland Company?

CHAPTER THREE

DEVELOPMENTS IN THE 1860s

MEANWHILE, new wagons were still being ordered, with 200 wagons being requested from the Metropolitan Co. on 13th January 1864 at £65 19s 6d each. These are recorded in a payment later on, showing their delivery:

14th June 1864 Metropolitan Railway Carriage and
Waggon Co:
100 New Low sided Goods Waggons, Nos. 3074 to
3173 delivered 12th April to 31st May   £6597 10s 0d

These were followed by the other 100, Nos. 3174 to 3273.

On 26th January 1864, the Engineer was instructed 'to prepare specifications and obtain tenders from the Metropolitan and the Midland Waggon Companies for ten Goods Break Vans', a process which apparently resulted in the later inclusion of the Oldbury Waggon Co. amongst the tenderers, and produced bids of £110 per van from the Midland, £125 from Oldbury, and £145 from the Metropolitan Co.; the Midland tender was accepted, and later modified to £114 per van. These 'Break Vans' were supplied eventually at £116 9s 9d each, and paid for in August. The Metropolitan Co. were then paid £815 10s 0d in October 1864 for repairing 20 old wagons, followed by 20 more in November, and another 20 in December. In the meantime, an additional travelling crane for accidents (at a cost not to exceed £375) was resolved upon in March 1864, but does not seem to have been ordered until February 1865; the builder was Bray, Waddington & Co. of Leeds.

The North Stafford then turned to Brown, Marshall & Co. for 74 new wagons at £63 15s 0d each, ordered in November 1864 and supplied in February 1865, followed by 54 more of the same order in April, and 33 in May, a total of 161 wagons. Bray, Waddington had serviced 34 wagons by May 1865, too, involving fairly substantial repairs at about £50 per wagon! Also in May, Edward Wilson was paid £105 for 'Inspecting Rolling Stock & Written Report Thereon'. A further 39 new wagons came from Brown, Marshall in April, paid for in May, making up the order to 200 wagons. The Midland Waggon Co. were paid for rebuilding 20 wagons in October, and it seems that this activity probably involved the earliest wagon stock of the NSR, now some 15 years old; no doubt it had been well used and, like the engine stock, was beginning to need some renewal by this time. Two cattle wagons were reported as being destroyed by fire in May 1864.

This burst of activity had increased the North Stafford's wagon stock from 2,167 at the end of 1861, to 2,411 by the end of 1863, and 3,974 in December 1868. A short period of tranquillity ensued, the next major investment in wagon stock not occurring until 1870, when a net increase of 490 wagons was recorded.

North Staffordshire Railway Rolling Stock Returns
From the 45th Half-Yearly Report, July 1868:

Return of Working Stock:

Engines & Tenders	78
Tank Engines	14
First Class Carriages	1
Family "	2
Composite "	66
Second Class "	22
Third " "	105
Horse Boxes	31
Dog Box	1
Carriage Trucks	18
Passenger Break Vans	27
Goods Break Vans	40
Covered Waggons	83
Goods and Mineral Waggons	3698
Cattle Waggons	112

The North Stafford apparently bought 250 wagons from Messrs. Adams in 1865, though quite what they were is in doubt, as in September 1870 they were detailed to be rebuilt as 6-ton wagons, charging the cost in excess of their then valuation at £34 each to capital account; the work was done by outside builders. At the same time, the urgent need for further wagons prompted a proposal for 200 new 8-ton wagons, to be built in the company's own shops. However, in October 1870, tenders for 100 wagons at £60 each from the 'Ashbury Company' and 100 at £69 9s 0d from the 'the Metropolitan Company' were accepted in addition to these. Further, in January 1871, 100 additional 6-ton wagons were ordered from the Metropolitan Co. in place of 100 of those to be built in the NSR shops.

Also in January 1871, the following was minuted: 'Additional Waggon Stock: Resolved that until further orders all 6-ton Waggons rebuilt be converted into 8-ton waggons and that a charge of £5 per ton be made against Capital account in respect of the increased value and carrying capacity of the Stock'.

In February 1871, the General Manager reported 'that 6 additional Goods Break Vans were required for working the new lines recently opened & Mr. Dodds was instructed to prepare for building them in the Shops of the Company'. Later that month, 200 additional wagons were ordered from the Metropolitan Co. at £60 9s 0d each. In October of that same year, 'the urgent necessity for a further addition to the wagon stock of the Company to meet the large increase in tonnage requiring conveyance' led to the company inviting tenders for 500 wagons 'similar to the last ordered and upon deferred payment'. This produced offers from the Gloucester Wagon Co., the Oldbury Wagon Co., the Metropolitan Wagon Co., Harrison & Camm, the Ashbury Co., the Birmingham Co. and Brown, Marshall & Co.; the Oldbury Co.'s tender was finally accepted, with deferred payments over seven years.

Plate 6.   Apedale Steelworks; in the foreground, behind the contrasting pair of Midland Coal, Coke & Iron Co. wagons, and attached to a Manning, Wardle 0-6-0T, is what may be an ex-NSR brake van of early pattern, without side lights, and possibly like early GWR and SDJR examples.

H. Minshull

The position of the North Stafford's rolling stock was apparently none too healthy by 1870, possibly due to the lull in new construction since 1865. This state of affairs was not made public until 1874 when, after 'misleading statements' at a meeting of the company on the 12th August of that year, T. W. Dodds (the former Resident Engineer) wrote a long letter which appeared in the columns of *The Staffordshire Daily Sentinel.* Dodds quoted several of his own letters to the company, including one to Percy Morris, the Company Secretary, dated 7th June 1870:

> '. . . I regret to say that we are in a very bad position with respect to damaged waggons, and further that I have seen, and still see, the position will become much worse, and that it will only be remedied by a heavy expenditure and a great push, as the waggons for some time have been cobbled up, or as the term here used, vamped up, and that the expenditure upon them has actually been thrown away . . . To bring the stock into the position shown in the last half year's report will require between 400 and 500 waggons making . . .'

Dodds reported the rolling stock position of the NSR at the end of 1870 as being:

Stock at the end of 1870		Stock, 1849	Change, (1849-1870)
6	First Class Carriages	—	+6
63	Composite Carriages	60	+3
22	Second class carriages	—	+22
92	Third class carriages	100	−8
31	Horse Boxes	40	−9
	(The 1 Dog Box which had appeared since 1849 had since disappeared during 1870!)		
18	Carriage Trucks	30	−12
27	Passenger Break Vans	20	+7
3612	Goods & Mineral Waggons	450	+3162
77	Covered Goods Waggons	50	+27
101	Cattle Waggons	100	+1
33	Coke Waggons	—	+33
108	Timber Waggons	—	+108
40	Goods Break Vans	—	+40
—	Sheep Vans	20	−20

CHAPTER FOUR

DEVELOPMENTS IN DESIGN AND CONSTRUCTION

T HE 1870 (and probably later) wagons from the Metropolitan Company are those illustrated by the surviving drawing of a goods wagon in the Metropolitan Cammell collection in Birmingham[15]. The notable feature of this design was the buffers. These were a combination of dumb and spring buffers in that the stocks were large baulks of timber, in part extensions of the solebars, which were bored longitudinally to take spring buffer heads and shanks, with the shanks taken through these holes to the central cross-members of the wagon frame and attached there to leaf springs running transversely. In appearance, these wagons looked like dumb-buffered vehicles converted partially to spring buffers, but they were quite new. The Furness Railway had some similar 'half and half' buffered wagons and vans, but it is not certain whether they were so built as new, or whether they were conversions[16]. The NSR wagons were 16ft 0in long over the body, 7ft 6in wide, with 3-plank (1ft 6in) sides, but 2-plank ends; the wheelbase was 9ft 7in. The sledge type brake (with a thick block) was fitted to one

side of the vehicle only. Five-link coupling chains were supplied, and the grease axle boxes were flat-based with 'NSR ⬡ 1870' on their front faces. The impression given by the drawing is that of a Metropolitan C & W design but incorporating some North Stafford parts, perhaps including the axle box castings. Unusually for a working drawing, the lettering is shown ('N.S.R', with only two, square stops) at the left-hand end of the wagon, in 3½ inch letters, on the middle plank. The Staffordshire Knot, 14½in long, was in the centre of the side, also on the middle plank, whilst 'TO CARRY 6 TONS', in 3in and 2½in upright letters was positioned at the right-hand end, again on the middle plank. As can be gathered from the minutes, several hundred wagons of this type were probably running on the North Stafford in the 'seventies and 'eighties, and one or two fragmentary views of them have survived. However, there are few indications as to their running numbers, though it is probable that a number were in the 4000 series (4855 being one such wagon definitely recorded). Mr. K. Werrett measured a

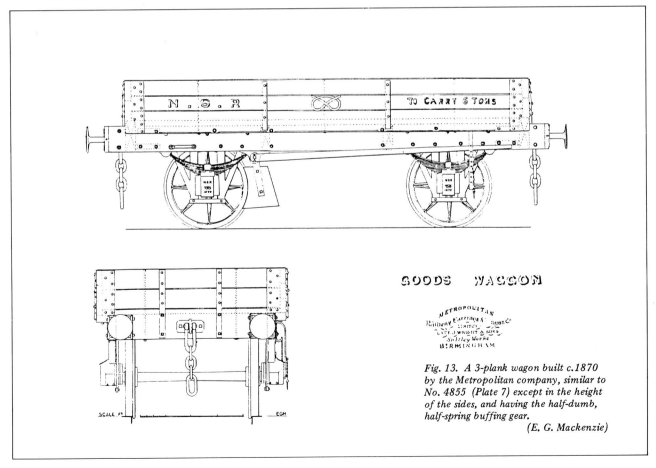

GOODS WAGGON

METROPOLITAN
Railway Carriages & Wagon Co
LATE J WRIGHT & SONS
Saltley Works
BIRMINGHAM

Fig. 13. A 3-plank wagon built c.1870 by the Metropolitan company, similar to No. 4855 (Plate 7) except in the height of the sides, and having the half-dumb, half-spring buffing gear.

(E. G. Mackenzie)

Plate 7. This view of the Bass & Co. Ale Banks at Shobnall, Burton-on-Trent, shows a rake of NSR wagons which comprise several of the types used for carrying ale casks, as well as being utilised for other, quite different traffic. It seems to have been taken in the early 1900s, as all the wagons carry the small lettering style; also, all six have brakes on one side only. Reading from left to right, details which can be discerned are: (1) No.4855, a 2-plank fixed side wagon with the half-dumb, half-spring buffers, 3-link couplings, flat-based grease axleboxes with the company's initials in the centre boss. Tare not visible; '8 Tons' in italic, right lower plank. Load is 21 smaller casks. (2) Lettering very faint: the number could be 956 (?), also 2-plank, but with the 'rubber' padded buffers on pads (probably remnants of dumb buffers); flat base axleboxes. Load is 18 casks. (3) Lettering very faint: 3-plank dropside, with lettering on the middle plank. Also has the 'rubber' buffers and flat base axleboxes. Load is 14 large casks. (4) No.2152, 2-plank. 'To carry 6(?) Tons' at right. Spring buffers with webbed shanks, axleboxes are flat-based. Load of small casks. (5) Number *might* be 272, with 'To Carry 6(?) Tons' following. One-plank, buffers not clear; grease axleboxes. (6) Indistinct; could be 3 or 4-plank, side door. Lettering on middle (?) plank. Possibly spring buffers. Load is a variety of cask sizes. In the background is a roofless cattle wagon, possibly NSR, no doubt also in use for cask traffic.

J. S. Simnett

Plate 8. For many years, most goods wagons had dumb buffers for economy, and it was only in the 1880s that the North Stafford began to provide its wagon stock with spring buffers on a general basis; indeed, dumb-buffered wagons were still running in departmental service (e.g. for locomotive coal) up to the Great War. This photograph shows 'D' class 0-6-0T No.140 at Uttoxeter in the 1890s, on a train of dumb-buffered wagons. The wagon nearest the engine (No.1056?) is 2-plank, has the round-base axleboxes, and presumably the single lever brake, one side only.

L&GRP,
cty. David & Charles

2-plank version of this wagon[17], apparently numbered 5114, which would seem to indicate a later (and possibly problematical) building date. This wagon had slightly different (but still flat-sided) axle boxes with bosses at the front, and Mr. Werrett shows the large NS and knot lettering, which would indicate a post-1912 survival (possibly as service stock?); quite a long-lived wagon! Mr. H. B. Holland records a similar 2-plank vehicle, No. 4262, with one brake shoe on one side visible, and lettered 'NSR ⚭ 4262' on the top plank with '8 Tons' in italic under the number; 'To Carry' is not written. This may be a c.1870/1 wagon, later upgraded to 8-tons capacity after January 1871.

A view datable to 1872 is of some interest, as it illustrates a wagon which has 'TO CARRY . . .' at the *left*-hand end of the wagon, and in upright letters; unfortunately the rest of the wagon cannot be seen, leaving unanswered the position of other lettering, the knot, and the number. Could this have been an earlier wagon, dating from the 1860s, or even the 1850s? This 3-plank wagon had dumb buffers and flat-bottomed axle boxes with a central boss, possibly like those of the Gloucester C & W Co. brake vans of 1874, to be described later.

Whilst on the topic of development in buffers, it does seem from various evidence that some conversion work was carried out at times. For example, the survival of the 1849 pattern of self-contained buffers on several vehicles

quite late in the nineteenth century (and even into the twentieth) may indicate the re-use of older buffers on previously dumb-buffered stock. Another example is wagon No. 2094 (number a little indistinct, but certainly in the 2000 series), photographed at Apedale Ironworks in, it is thought, the 1870s. The vehicle is apparently new; it is clean inside, and had been newly painted. The fat, self-contained buffers reappear on this vehicle, a 3-plank wagon with the sledge brake, and the buffers were mounted on a wooden pad (or reduced dumb buffers?). The lettering here is similar to that on the 1870 Metropolitan C & W drawing, but the number appears on the bottom plank immediately below the knot, and below this again, painted on the solebar. If the number quoted is correct, this might be one of a batch built somewhere between 1857 and 1862, just possibly with the padded buffers from new, though the clean condition is difficult to explain if this building date was correct − unless the photograph is earlier than stated.

Dumb-buffered wagons were probably in use on the NSR from its earliest years, as they were with other railway companies and private owners; at that time, only vans and special types of stock were thought to merit spring buffers. With privately-owned wagons, the 1887 RCH specification[18] heralded the eventual demise of the dumb-buffered vehicle, though this specification itself did allow their continued construction. The Gloucester Carriage & Wagon Company, for example, did not build

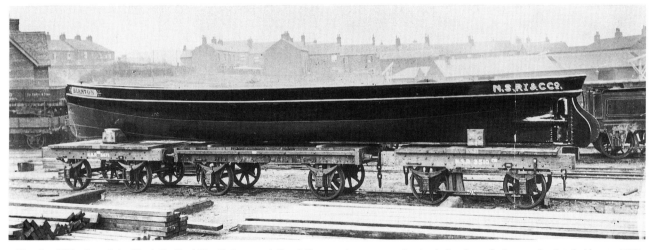

Plate 8a. This view of the North Staffordshire Railway and Canal Company's steam tug *Barnton*, hull only, at Stoke, may be dated either to 1879 when a new hull for No.1 Steam Tug was built at a cost of £350, or alternatively to 1877, when W. Smith supplied No.3 Steam Tug at a cost of £820 less £250 for the old boat which it replaced. The former seems the most likely. The hull is supported by two Boiler Trucks, Nos.3471 and 3510: singles, not twins, with dumb buffers, sledge brake one side only, flat-bottomed grease axleboxes, and a simple flat top to the wagon without any surrounding coping or edge-piece. These are similar to the K. Werrett drawing of a Timber Truck, No.2658, originally of 1862, below solebars, except for the tie-bars between the axleboxes. The wagon numbers are painted on the solebars, and no knot appears here, although there are knots and NSR on the axleboxes; these two wagons seem to be unpainted otherwise. Possibly they are newly-built and pressed into service for this particular occasion before being painted. The middle vehicle is extremely interesting and bears an oval numberplate (156) not recorded on any other vehicle. Although it also has the 1870 axleboxes and is fitted with spring buffers, it could conceivably be the original wagon 156 modernised by these additions; or alternatively it may demonstrate a thrifty use of an older numberplate? It has 5-link coupling chains, but no brakes, suggesting that it spent most of its time in such Departmental use, rather than running use, unless it worked as part of a coupled set? However, it is not apparently coupled up to the two boiler trucks in this view. The wagon at the top left appears to be identical to that of the Metropolitan RC & W Co. drawing of 1870 in having the half-and-half dumb/spring buffers (the shank can just be seen), and also displaying the *upright* lettering for the tonnage indication. The number cannot be made out, but is likely to be in the 3500 − 4500+ bracket. A pair of the self-contained 'Rubber' buffers can be seen by *Barnton's* bows, on two wagons. The tender on the right seems to be of c.1855-60 vintage, possibly from a Kitson 0-6-0.   *Manifold Collection*

any more dumb-buffered PO wagons after this time, though the prohibition of their use (except for Departmental work) did not eventuate until 1913. So, it is more probable that the surviving NSR diagram 6 (for a 6-ton, 1-plank wagon of 9ft wheelbase, being 14ft 6in long and 7ft wide with 11in sides) represents a dumb-buffered wagon of at least 1865 origin, if not earlier. Such wagons may have been built over a long period in virtually the same form, and latterly without much alteration except for spring buffers and a gradual improvement of the braking system.

To return to the minutes, a pause in wagon matters is indicated until 1874, when an estimate of £46 per wagon was submitted 'for rebuilding 50 six-ton wagons with dead buffers to replace broken-up stock' in the NSR Shops. In the same month, a tender from the Gloucester Waggon Company for 10 new goods brake vans was accepted at £202 each; this was, seemingly, a high price for the time, and one speculates on the reasons for whatever change in ordering policy, or innovations in design or construction, were involved. These brake vans are illustrated by the well-known works photograph of No. 60[19]. A 'return of wagons under repair' for February 1874 showed that 177

needed heavy restoration work, 114 required light repairs, and that 278 had been broken up; this state of affairs brought a sharp reprimand for the Foreman of the Waggon Department. Thus, on 10th February 1874, a tender from the Gloucester Waggon Company 'for rebuilding broken up goods wagons' at £46 10s 0d each was accepted. The 150 vehicles involved were delivered in three equal lots in July 1874, January 1875, and July 1875, the NSR finding wheels, axles, and springs. In December of that year, tenders for 100 additional wagons were invited from the Gloucester Company, The Birmingham Wagon Co., the Metropolitan Company, and Clay of Derby.

During 1875 (and later), the emphasis appears to have been on carriage stock, though in October, the General Manager was instructed to notify the Waggon Foreman 'that all waggons broken up must be rebuilt, regard being had to the minimum number of wagons which can be built with economy'. In June, there had been a report on the condition of the 29 horse boxes owned by the company, and the foreman was instructed 'to have the ten horse boxes now in bad order thoroughly repaired before the commencement of the hunting season'.

A TYPICAL NORTH STAFFORD WAGON: ITS REPAIR AND DEMISE

The career of what may have been a not untypical North Stafford goods wagon of the second half of the nineteenth century can be told in some detail, from 1864 to its demise on 16th July 1907, some 43 years of service[20]. Wagon No. 2995 was stated to have been built in October 1864 by the Metropolitan Carriage & Waggon Company at Saltley, Birmingham, though the NSR minutes[21] seem to suggest it was delivered six months earlier, in March/April 1864, as one of an order of 100 low-sided wagons, Nos. 2974-3073. It was of 6-ton capacity, with a tare of 4 tons 8 cwt. (in 1907). At an Inquiry into an accident on the Great Central Railway at Waleswood (between Sheffield and Worksop) during 1907, Joseph Hickman, Carriage and Waggon Inspector of the NSR, gave evidence as to the career of No. 2995, which was involved in that accident:

1878	Heavy Repairs
1881	Heavy Repairs
1884	Heavy Repairs
1890	Light Repairs
1891	Light Repairs
1893	Fitted with two new headstocks
1897	Lifted, and fitted with new axle boxes, brasses, and two new axle guards
1899	Fitted with four repaired buffers, 'rubber buffers' – (presumably those of the c.1850 large 'padded' pattern); No. 2995 had probably been dumb-buffered until this time
1903	Heavy Repairs
1907	(26th January) Lifted, axle guards reset, two new brasses fitted, brake adjusted

The springs were not secured to the spring shoes at any time, but simply slid along them, as on most NSR wagons built prior to 1878; after that time, a securing bolt was normally fitted to each shoe of new vehicles. The springs of No. 2995 were (or were identical to) those provided in 1864.

In the accident on 16th July 1867, No. 2995 apparently buffer-locked with CLC wagon No. 3335, thus causing the disintegration of a pair of its axle guards, the breaking of an axle, the parting of its train (a GCR goods), and interference with a passenger train on the adjoining line. It had been inspected earlier that day by a GCR wagon examiner and, though old, was considered to be in a satisfactory condition.

The history of No. 2995 is reminiscent of the cricket bat that had received three new blades and two new handles, but was still the same bat! Most goods wagons of the time must have similarly undergone very many repairs, replacements, and conversions, and the NSR seems to have been very thriftily-minded in the upkeep of its stock in this manner. The photograph of wagon No. 2949 (*Plate 5*), being conveyed on the Leek and Manifold Valley Railway in 1904, shows its condition at that time, and may reflect the final state of No. 2995, including the buffer conversion.

CHAPTER FIVE

THE 1880s AND 1890s: THE LUKE LONGBOTTOM ERA

Plate 9. In this view of Ashbourne Yard (c.1880), roofless cattle wagons are included in the train on the left, headed by 0-6-0 No.100 (Robert Stephenson & Co., 1860) and are sheeted to give some protection to their occupants. Noteworthy are the three-way point, and the use of very short rails: 7 chairs per rail length! *Manifold Collection*

AT the half-yearly General Meeting of the company on 3rd February 1882, the Chairman, Colin Minton Campbell, reported: 'we are going through our rolling stock very systematically, and replacing the old rolling stock, much of which has been on the line ever since it has been in existence, by rolling stock of more modern requirements'. Sixty more wagons were said to have been built in the past half year than in the previous half year, though the minutes are silent about this construction. Nonetheless, the period of Luke Longbottom's tenure at Stoke was to be associated with a thoroughgoing attempt to bring the North Stafford's mechanical engineering affairs completely up-to-date.

Longbottom came to Stoke as Locomotive Superintendent in 1882 from the L & NWR, where he had spent some 22 years service. His new Carriage & Waggon Works Manager, R. Dent, had also spent a similar length of time with the same company, at Wolverton. It is not surprising, therefore, that some of the ideas and likenesses of the Premier Line's products became visible at Stoke-on-Trent after this time, when the workshops there really began to come into their own as designers and producers of railway rolling stock.

The new Locomotive Superintendent seems to have concentrated on extending and improving the engine stock of the North Staffordshire for the first few years after his arrival, making considerable increases in standardisation, and laying the foundations of a suitable and up-to-date series of engine types for both goods and passenger work. However, in 1885, Mr. Longbottom turned his attention to goods rolling stock, and reported to the Traffic and Finance Committee with estimates for rebuilding 6, 8 and 10-ton wagons: it was then decided to adopt the 8-ton wagon as the standard wagon for the NSR.

A period of activity, building milk vans, then ensued, a small but almost continuous ten-year stream of work from the NSR Shops; it is convenient to consider these orders together. In February 1886, two new vans were ordered at £195 each, followed by two 'proposed new Milk Vans', also at £195, in August 1887. Two new 'Milk Trucks' were then ordered in July 1888, followed by a batch of six (at £200 each) in November 1888; the six additional vans ordered in August 1890 were to cost £190 each, though. Then, in October 1893, six more milk vans at £190 each were ordered, and a further six in May 1895, also at £190.

Plate 10. NSR No.481, an 8-ton, 3-plank dropside wagon (possibly with 27in. sides) bearing all the hallmarks of an early Longbottom design of the 1880s, photographed here in Jimmy's Yard, Oakamoor, c.1905, in use as a platform for a Whitsuntide preacher. It seems to be generally covered by the later Diagram 5, which was for a 9ft wheelbase wagon, 15ft 6in by 7ft 0in inside, 18ft 0in over buffers, except that the wheelbase was more likely to be 9ft 7in. Tare is not shown, but a similar 2-plank dropside with 21in sides would be about 5.11.3. These dropside wagons seem to have been made with a number of side heights, 2 or 3 planks, up to 27 inches.

J. W. Walker

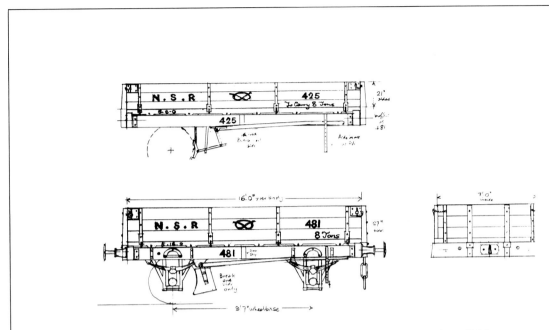

Fig. 14. A similar 3-plank wagon with 21in sides, 9ft 7in wheelbase, and tare 5.6.0, was measured by Guy Hemingway in NSR livery as late as 1929. This was NSR No. 425 which, like 481, presumably bore the number of an older, scrapped wagon. Both of these vehicles had the round-based grease axleboxes and the later, unwebbed pattern of buffer casting. The sledge brake one side only, was fitted to 481, whereas No. 425 was provided with one of the later push-rod variety, to both sides. The headstock ends function as doorstops, being canted back to suit the fall of the wagon sides. NSR No. 323 was similar in being a 3-plank dropside, but was of only 6-ton capacity. It had the same pattern buffers as Nos. 425 and 481 when recorded, but only the earlier, flat-based axleboxes. (Author; Author/G. Hemingway)

All these seem to have been four-wheeled types, possibly with slight detail differences, for in July 1896, 'Six New 6-wheeled Milk Vans' costing £260 each were ordered to be built, 'to hold 64 Milk Cans each'; drawings of these new six-wheeled types have survived. A presumed accident was reported to the Traffic and Finance Committee on 2nd March 1897, involving damage to milk van No. 361 at Market Drayton; there was no further explanation in the minutes. A further six new milk vans were ordered on 23rd January 1906, now at £250 each.

North Staffordshire Milk Vans: Running Numbers

Four-wheel type:
    325 (of 1889)
    332 (of 1890)
    333-335 (of 1891)
    0174-0176 (of 1892)
    181, 189, 194, 195, 199, 0177, 0179 (of 1893)
    344-349 (of 1894)
    350-355 (of 1895)

Six-wheel type:
    357-359 (of 1896)
    196, 360-362 (of 1897)

Possibly four-wheel types:
    310, 311, 314-317, 375-380 (of 1906)
    056, 057 060 (of 1907)
    0303, 0304, 0318, 0319 (of 1908)
    294, 296, 301, 0302, 0315 (of 1909)

Meanwhile, Mr. Longbottom was also building a small number of covered carriage trucks at Stoke. The first reference is on 5th March 1895, when: 'The plan was approved and the Truck ordered to be built at a cost of £240'. 'The plan' has survived[22] but no view of such a CCT (No. 21) has been found. Another vehicle was ordered on 21st October 1902: 'The Plan as submitted was approved & the Truck ordered to be built at a cost of £230', but this order was increased to two trucks on 30th December 1902, at £235 each. A further carriage truck was ordered on 28th July 1903. These latter three vehicles were Nos. 1, 22 and 23.

Small numbers of horse boxes were also being built in the NSR shops. Six vehicles were ordered in February 1898, to be built during that year (at £260 each) with a further three being approved in July 1898 for a total of £740. The boxes built at this time were Nos. 28-33 of 1898, and Nos. 02, 03, 05, 06, 023, 024 of 1900. Four horse boxes were to be rebuilt from July 1901 at a cost of £261 each. Surviving Stoke drawing Nos. 1946 and 1947 show a side elevation, plan, and sections of the elliptical roof version of the NSR horse box; however, their annotation as 'Copy DGs' and the use of grease axle boxes suggest that these 1912 drawings are, in fact, re-issues of the 1898 version.

NSR HORSE BOX TO DIAGRAM 1

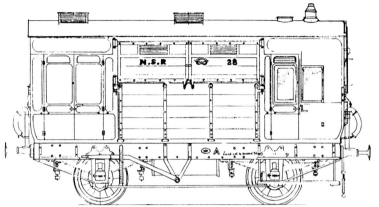

12ft 0in wheelbase

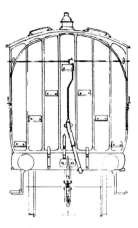

Elevation of Groom's
Compartment End:
Arc Roof type only

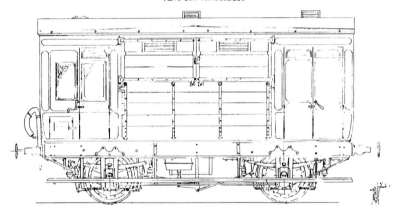

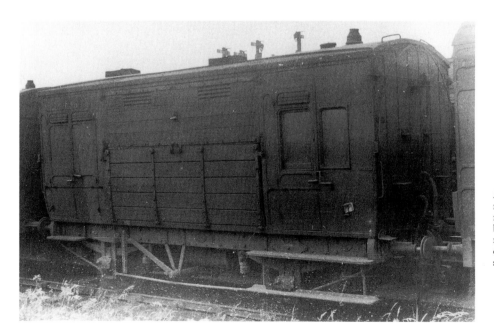

Plate 10a. Ex-NSR arc-roof horse-box with replacement oil axle-boxes. Note oil pot, also roof steps and rails at compartment end, also steam indicator.

R. Pochin

Plate 10b. Ex-NSR No.1, built 1913, shown here as LMS 43722. This vehicle was withdrawn in 1932. Note the roof steps and handrails at fodder compartment end, but alarm at the other.
F. W. Shuttleworth

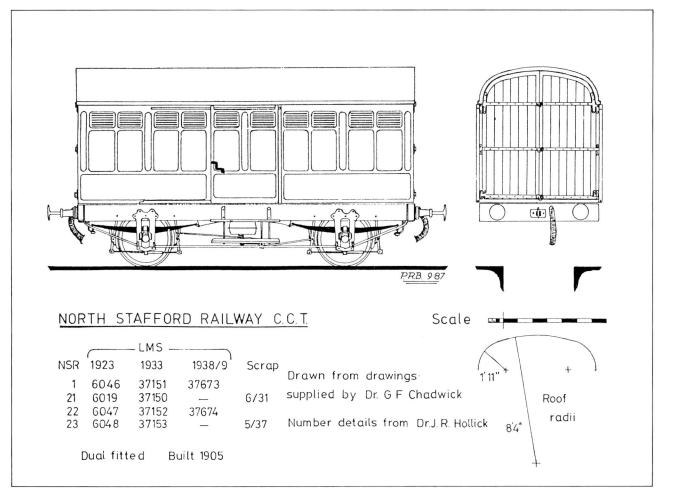

P.R.B. 9.87

NORTH STAFFORD RAILWAY C.C.T.

Scale

NSR	LMS			Scrap
	1923	1933	1938/9	
1	6046	37151	37673	
21	6019	37150	—	6/31
22	6047	37152	37674	
23	6048	37153	—	5/37

Drawn from drawings supplied by Dr. G F Chadwick

Number details from Dr. J. R. Hollick

Dual fitted   Built 1905

1'11"

Roof radii

8'4"

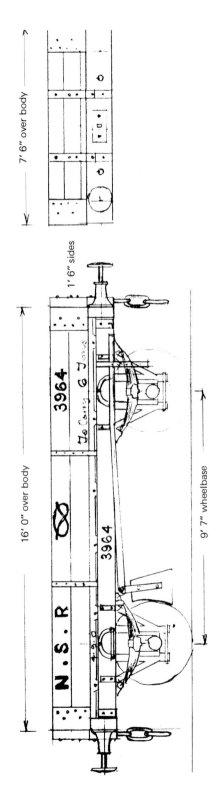

Fig. 15. NSR No. 3964: a 6-ton 2-plank wagon built c.1880-1890 with spring buffers, three-link couplings and the single-lever brake both sides. This wagon was measured by Guy Hemingway in 1928, still in NSR livery.

(Author)

7' 6" over body

1' 6" sides

16' 0" over body

9' 7" wheelbase

N.S.R

3964

To Carry 6 Tons

3964

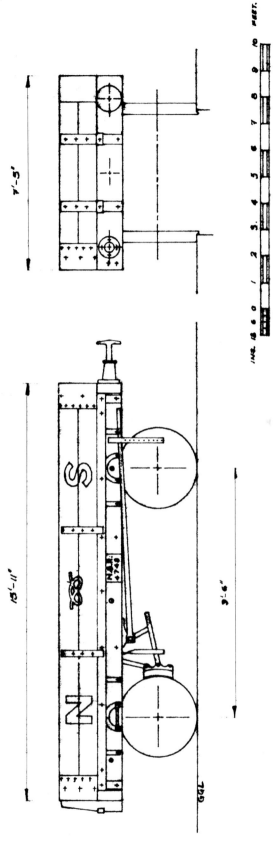

Fig. 16. Another 2-plank wagon, probably the most popular type, used by the North Stafford for a variety of traffic. No. 4748 was probably built in the 1880s, and carries the later type of single-lever brake with push-rod, but now fitted on both sides (see Plate 11).

(G. G. Lines, for HMRS)

4' · 5'

15'—11"

3'-6"

7d6

N.S

N

N.S.
4748

INS. 1860 1 2 3 4 5 6 7 8 9 10 FEET.

Plate 11. Two-plank open No.4748 again; fitted with single-lever brake and push rod (both sides), Longbottom grease axleboxes, and 3-link couplings. The vehicle sports the post-1912 lettering style, with the cast numberplate on the solebar.

J. P. Richards

Plate 12. LMS (ex-NSR) 8-ton, 2-plank open wagon No.193134, photographed in a later condition on 29th April 1939.   *R. J. Essery*

Plate 13. The end view of LMS No.193134; 29th April 1939.   *R. J. Essery*

Plate 14. End, side and interior view of NSR 2-plank wagon 4520 in later lettering style but still with the single-lever brake and grease axleboxes.

HMRS

Plate 15. NSR 2-plank No.940 displays the late wagon livery, without 'knot', c.1920. The wagon is fitted with grease, round-based axleboxes. *F. W. Shuttleworth Collection*

Returning to open wagons, at the end of December 1889, 30 new 10-ton vehicles were bought from the Phoenix Company, followed by another 30 from the same source in October 1890, at £62 10s 0d each, less 2½% discount for cash, delivered in three weeks. These were followed in December 1891 by 200 8-ton goods wagons from the NSR regular suppliers, the Metropolitan C & W Co., at £63 15s 0d per wagon, being delivered in June and July 1892. Drawings of these wagons survive from several sources.

Two new travelling cranes were also ordered at this time: an 8-ton crane for the Engineer's Dept. (at £410) from Cowan and Sheldon, and a 30 cwt crane for Milton at £90, both in June 1892. In February 1895 a further new steam breakdown crane was ordered from Cowan & Sheldon at a cost of £1,550, being delivered to Stoke.

In October 1890 and March 1894, there was an interesting transaction involving 50, then a further 25, second-hand open wagons, these being obtained from Stanier & Co. They were followed in November 1895 by a further 25 (at a total cost of £400), with another 25 in December, at a total of £265. Stanier was an ironmaster, and also Deputy Chairman of the NSR Finance Committee, and it may be that these were iron-bodied wagons which the 'Knotty' used extensively for locomotive coal, though earlier vehicles for this use may have been obtained as far back as the private wagon purchases of 1864, probably from Robert Heath (from where 61 wagons were obtained). There is later evidence that the NSR made use of second-hand wagons (with dumb buffers) for loco coal, as distances carried were very short, and public carriage was not involved with these wagons.

In October 1896, Longbottom was ordered to build 100 new goods vans at £95 each by October 1897, but this order was amended to 50 vans only from the NSR shops, and 50 were ordered from the Metropolitan Company at £99 each in November, with delivery promised in 15 weeks. An interesting proposal was made in October 1897, in which the company would build 100 wagons for iron bar traffic during 1898, 'according to the plan furnished', at £60 each; the plan, alas, has disappeared. In November 1897, 100 new 8-ton wagons were ordered from the company's shops, and tenders for wheels and axles, ironwork, and oak scantling were accepted by the committee. At the same time, 40 wagons were hired from the Midland Carriage & Wagon Co. at £7 10s 0d per annum.

Orders for 1898 included three 8-ton wagons in October for the Permanent Way Dept. (at £65 10s 0d each) to a plan by Longbottom, now lost, and 100 new goods wagons at £60 each, also from Stoke Shops, tenders for the supply of ironwork and wheels being accepted in November.

1899 was a busy year for wagon orders. First of all, 50 of the new wagons ordered in the previous November were to be fitted with Williams sheet supports at £7 12s 0d per wagon, the only recorded use of sheet supports on the NSR. Then, also in January, 50 more locomotive coal wagons were to be hired on the best of terms, though whether these were to be wooden or iron wagons is not known. March saw 25 second-hand ballast wagons purchased at £26 each. In April, Mr. Leach's offer of seven goods vans at £56 each was accepted, though an offer of 10 vans, apparently second-hand, at £65 10s 0d each was not taken up. In September, Longbottom was

Plate 16. A view of Podmore Hall Colliery, Halmer End, c.1895. The waiting wagons include NSR 5-plank wagon No.5621, with rounded ends and dumb buffers; 3-plank No.127, newly painted and clean inside, with spring buffers, brakes one side only (possibly a new Longbottom standard wagon of 1891); a low iron wagon with spring buffers (which is not marked for 'Loco' coal); and another 5-plank, No.5298, with dumb buffers. Beyond, the end of another 4 or 5-plank loco coal wagon with dumb buffers can be seen, whilst another iron wagon with spring buffers is visible in the furthest batch.

W. Jack

able to report the completion of the 100 wagons ordered in November 1898, whereupon he was instructed to supply plans and estimates for a further 100. This he did in October, when 100 8-ton wagons at £71 10s 0d each were ordered from the company's shops. Also in October, it was resolved to purchase 40 wagons currently on hire from the Midland Carriage & Wagon Co., this number being increased later to 80 at £27 10s 0d each. Finally, in November, Longbottom was instructed to build eight new wagons for the Engineering Dept. at £78 each.

THE 1891 STANDARD WAGONS

Two Stoke drawings of 1891, Nos. 139 and 145, show the eventual adoption as standard for the NSR of spring buffers and V-hanger brakes, although the latter were still applied to both wheels on one side only. Grease axle boxes with rounded bases were now also standard. One of these wagons was illustrated by a drawing in the *Railway Engineer* the following year[23]. The buffer castings at this time had webs or flanges, and were flattened on top to form a footstep; however, a plain casting later replaced it. These wagons were later to be illustrated by Diagrams 2 and 3 respectively in the Wagon Diagram Book. Dia 2 covered an 8-ton/2-plank fixed-side wagon with a 10ft 5in wheelbase, and Dia 3 an 8-ton/3-plank side door wagon (with rounded ends) on a 9ft 7in wheelbase. Both diagrams covered a variety of lengths and tares, from 15ft 6in to 17ft, and tares of 5t 1cwt 3qtr to 5t 19cwt 3qtr in the case of Diagram 2 (with sides from 15½in to 21in high), whilst Diagram 3 covered lengths of 14ft 6in to 17ft, and tares from 5t 6cwt 0qtr to 6t 2cwt 0qtr (sides 27in high). It is quite possible that older types of wagon were covered by the same diagram.

Such wagons as these of 1891 represented quite the most up-to-date wagon building practice of the time – Luke Longbottom was a member of the RCH committee on wagon design and construction. The lettering of the wagons continued as in previous practice in general, although 'To Carry' was dropped at some time from the load indication. A batch of these wagons was built by the Metropolitan Carriage & Wagon Co. Ltd. in 1892, Order No. 948A; a relevant drawing survives.

Plate 17. In 1891, Longbottom produced a 2-plank, 8-ton wagon, 17ft 6in over headstocks by 7ft 5in wide, on a 10ft 5in wheelbase. Constructionally, no new features appeared on these wagons, except for the V-hanger brakes, again one side only, and the plain buffer castings. The round-base grease axleboxes were fitted. A variation of this design, presumably an earlier one, had the later pattern of push-rod style of single-lever brake, fitted both sides, as on wagon 4748. This photograph shows ex-NSR No.6216, tare 5.12.0, to this design by Longbottom, and built in 1902.
National Railway Museum

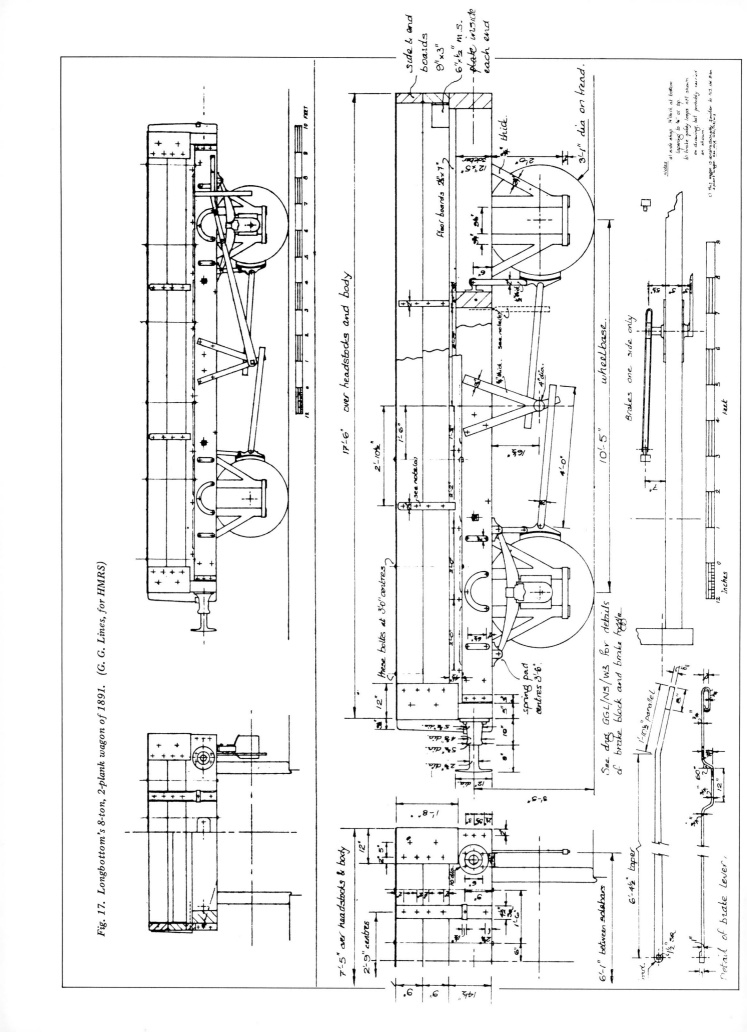

Fig. 17. Longbottom's 8-ton, 2-plank wagon of 1891. (G. G. Lines, for HMRS)

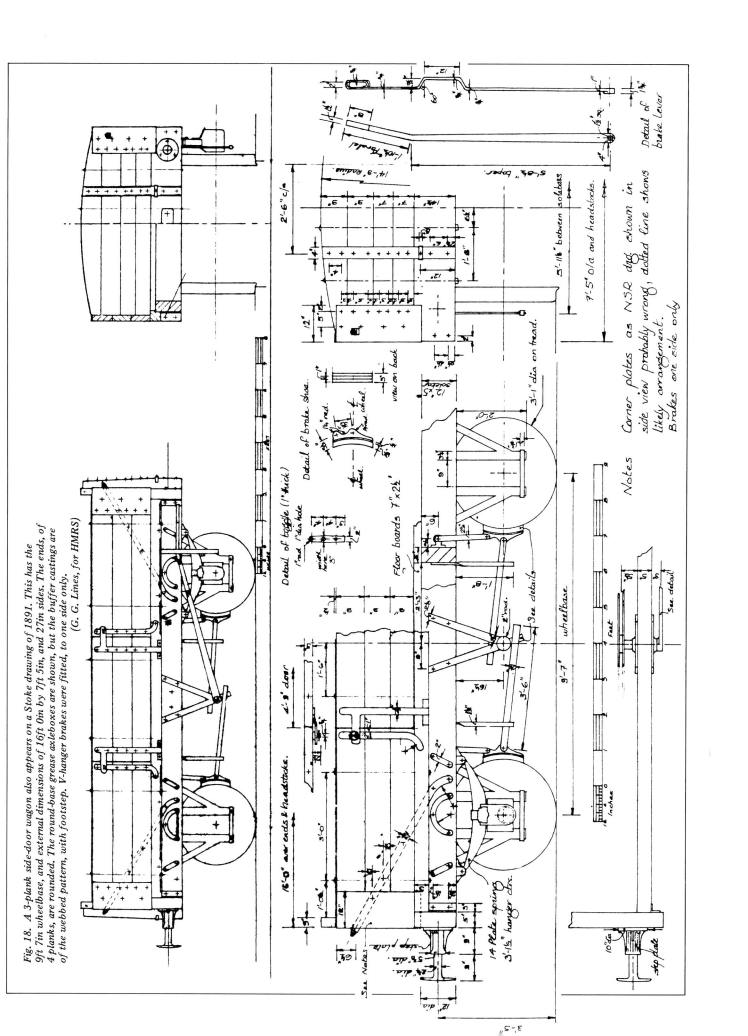

Fig. 18. A 3-plank side-door wagon also appears on a Stoke drawing of 1891. This has the 9ft 7in wheelbase, and external dimensions of 16ft 0in by 7ft 5in, and 27in sides. The ends, of 4 planks, are rounded. The round-base grease axleboxes are shown, but the buffer castings are of the webbed pattern, with footstep. V-hanger brakes were fitted, to one side only.

(G. G. Lines, for HMRS)

Plate 18. NSR No.5547, an 8 ton van, is seen at Bollington (on the Macclesfield, Bollington and Marple Railway) c.1900, in a rake of coal wagons. The Stirrup & Pye, Adderley Green Collieries, Stoke on Trent, wagons have dumb buffers, and carry numbers 53, 58 and 40; the other wagons belong to Joseph Welch, Coal Merchant, of Macclesfield.

Basil Jeuda

CHAPTER SIX

THE LAST YEARS OF MR LONGBOTTOM'S WORK AT STOKE

IN 1900, only one wagon transaction was recorded – Hurst Nelson's offer of 30 apparently second-hand wagons at £55 each being accepted. In March 1901, an instruction was given that all wagons for rebuilding should be converted to 10 tons, and later in that year that tenders for wagon wheels and axles were to be invited, as were tenders for wagon hire. Fifty second-hand wagons for locomotive coal were to be purchased in December at £25 each, subject to inspection. At the same meeting, what was no doubt the joint largest wagon order ever placed by the North Stafford was confirmed: 500 wagons at £66 3s 0d each from Metropolitan Carriage & Wagon Co., to be delivered at a rate of 25 wagons per month, commencing 1st April 1902. There is evidence that this batch of wagons included running numbers in the 6100 series, as Nos. 6103 and 6176 were photographed in 1904 in connection with either-side brake trials by the RCH, 6103 being at Edge Hill in April of that year. Both 6103 and 6176 were 10-ton, 2-plank wagons, with round-based grease axle boxes bearing the date 1902, and 6176 carried a Metropolitan RC & WC maker's plate on the solebar. V-hanger brakes were fitted one side only, i.e. one wheel on each axle being braked; 6103 had an NSR 'Either-side Break', and 6176 had 'J. Stone & Co.'s Patent Either-side Break'. Such brakes could be applied from either side of the wagon, but were not necessarily four-wheel brakes. Three other wagons of similar design in this series, Nos. 6164, 6286, and 6346 (?) are to be seen in *Plate 2* of Uttoxeter goods yard at some time circa 1905-1910[24].

Further purchases of wheels and axles were also authorised in 1901, and 25 covered goods wagons were ordered from the NSR shops, to be supplied over 18 months, at £95 each. Finally, on 17th December 1901, 50 wagons were purchased from the Midland Co. at £24 (instead of £25).

In May 1903, a reference to 'proposed 20-ton wagons for limestone traffic' was made, though these do not seem to have materialised.

What appears to be the first building of timber wagons for 40 years is recorded in 1900, with Stoke Shops supplying two pairs of twin bolster trucks at £148 7s 0d per pair, followed by an order for 10 pairs (at £137 10s 0d per pair) at the end of 1901. Drawings of these twin bolsters have survived[25].

BRAKE VANS

Meanwhile, building of 'goods break vans' by the NSR Workshops had been proceeding steadily for a number of years; the orders were as follows:

6	'extra' vans Jan 89	£180 each	
6	new pattern Dec 90	"	"
6	Dec 93	"	"
6	Oct 96	"	"
4	Jul 98	"	"
11	Apr 99	"	"
6	Dec 99	£192 each	
6	Dec 00	£190 each	
10	Nov 01	"	"

The 'new pattern' brake vans ordered in December 1890 appear to have resulted from the Board of Trade Inspector's recommendations following the spectacular crash of an NSR goods train at Uttoxeter on 11th October 1890[26]. In evidence, it was stated that the brake van on the goods train involved weighed only 8 tons 3 cwt, and this on a 422-ton train of 36 wagons. The Inspector recommended that there should be 'at least one 10-ton Break Van for every 20 waggons in a train, or part of 20.' As the maximum permitted length of a mineral train on the NSR at this time was 40 wagons, it followed that either two 10-ton brakes or one 20-ton brake would be required for a train of above average or maximum composition. The building of both 10-ton and 20-ton brake vans was a natural consequence of the acceptance of this recommendation, and this outcome would be the basis for the surviving Diagrams 11 and 20, of a nominally 10-ton and 20-ton brake van respectively. The diagrams illustrate the main features of the two types of 'break van', whilst more detailed constructional information can be derived from two relevant drawings which remain: Stoke No. 68 of 1888, and No. 1674 of 1908.

The comparative dimensions of the two brake van types were:

	Diagram 11	Diagram 20
Tare weight	11t 10cwt	20t 17cwt
Length over buffers	19ft 0in	21ft 0in
Length over body	16ft 0in	18ft 0in
Width	7ft 6in	7ft 8½in
Height from rail	10ft ½in	10ft 9½in
Height of body	6ft 5in	6ft 6in
Wheelbase	9ft 7in	10ft 0in

The 20-ton van was therefore 26% greater in volume than the 10-ton version, and its extra size, as well as bigger frame and ironwork, added to its greater weight. A comparison between the 1888 and 1908 Stoke drawings is instructive. Beginning with the frame, the main members were increased from 5in x 12in in the former to 5in x 13in and 6in x 13in in the latter, the solebars being faced with

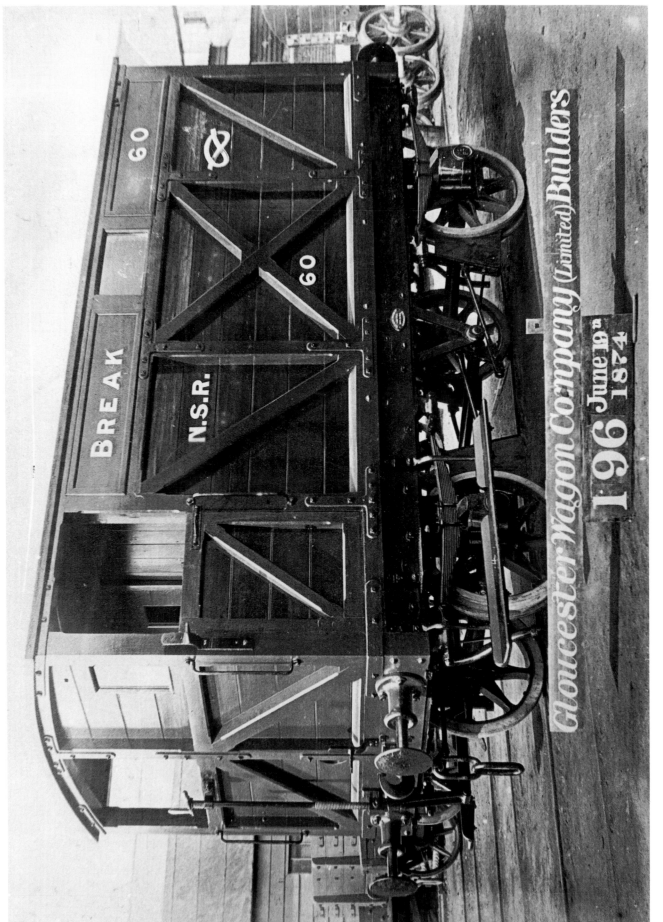

Plate 19. Gloucester C & W Co. brake van No.60 of 1874, the single side light design, later to the 10-ton standard. The external brake spindle and linkage, with central V-hanger (like a wagon), can be seen. *HMRS*

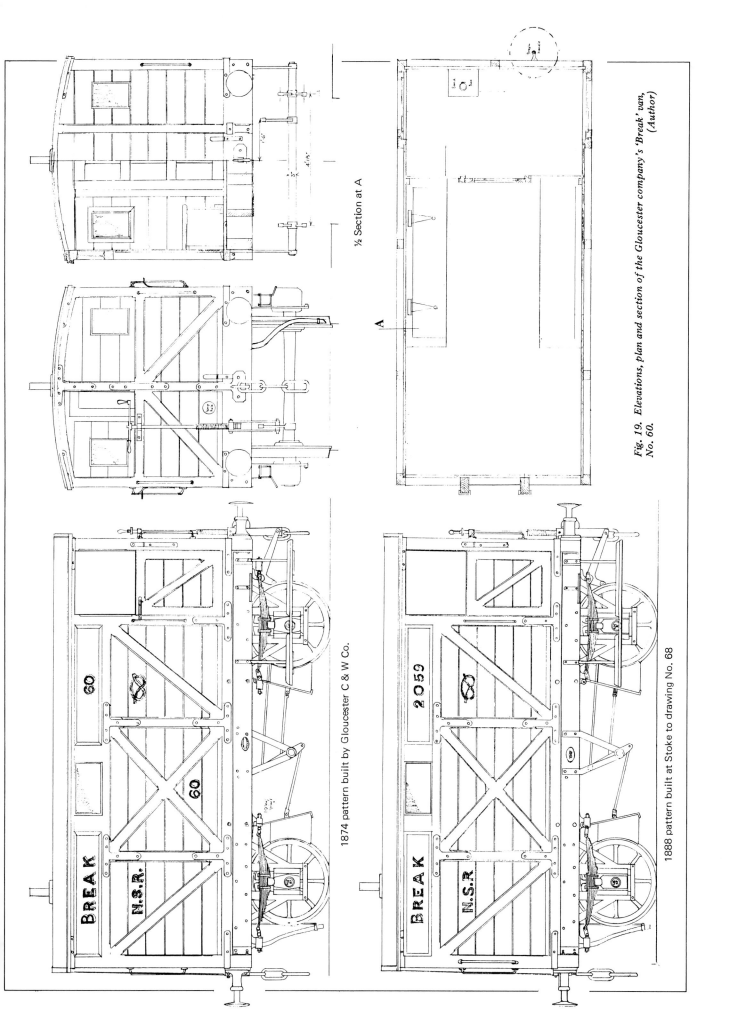

½ Section at A

Fig. 19. Elevations, plan and section of the Gloucester company's 'Break' van, No. 60.
(Author)

1874 pattern built by Gloucester C & W Co.

1888 pattern built at Stoke to drawing No. 68

Plate 20. An unidentified (possibly No.3057) brake van at Crewe (North Stafford), with LNWR 2-4-0 No.1120 *Apollo* nearby, pre-1905. A single-light van, this has the self-contained rubber buffers.   *A.G.Ellis*

Plate 21. A 10-ton brake van as running in 1913, with two sidelights, heavy frame strapping, but with the older centre V-hanger brake gear.
Locomotive Publishing Co.

Plate 22. NSR brake vans at Derby (North Stafford) siding, c.1890. No.459 is a 10-ton van, but has two sidelights and a central vertical hanger type of brake arrangement, also heavy strapping to the joints of the outside framing and a heavy tiebar between the axleguards. No.2091 is a single sidelight, 10-ton type.
Brian Radford

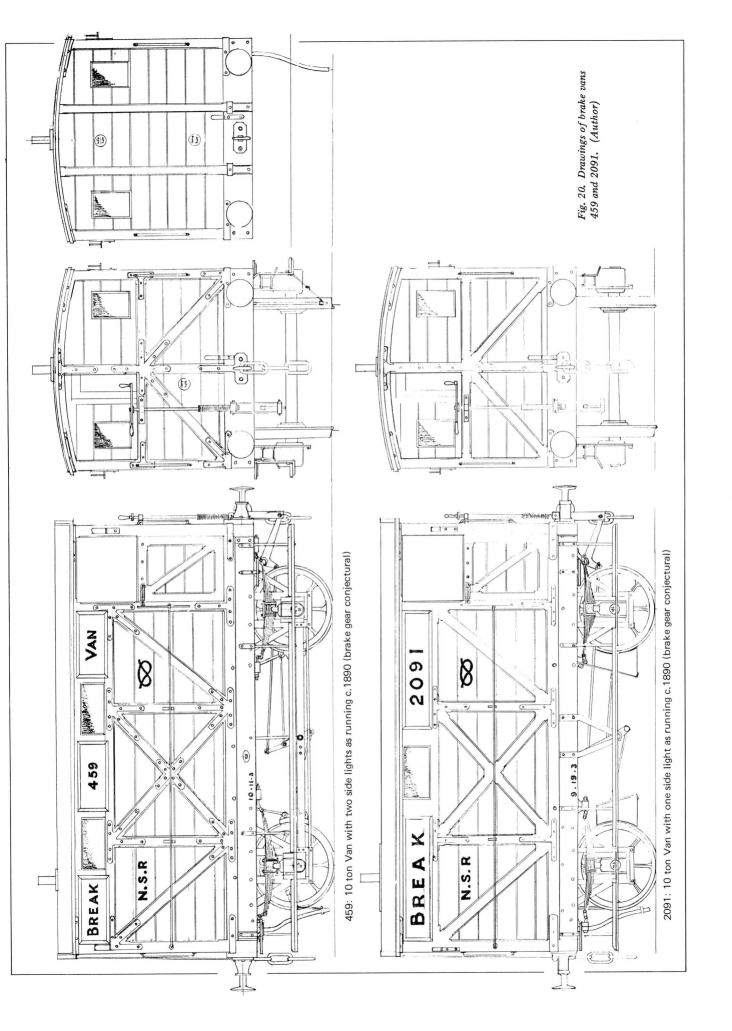

BREAK VAN 459 N.S.R

459: 10 ton Van with two side lights as running c.1890 (brake gear conjectural)

BREAK 2091 N.S.R

2091: 10 ton Van with one side light as running c.1890 (brake gear conjectural)

Fig. 20. Drawings of brake vans 459 and 2091. (Author)

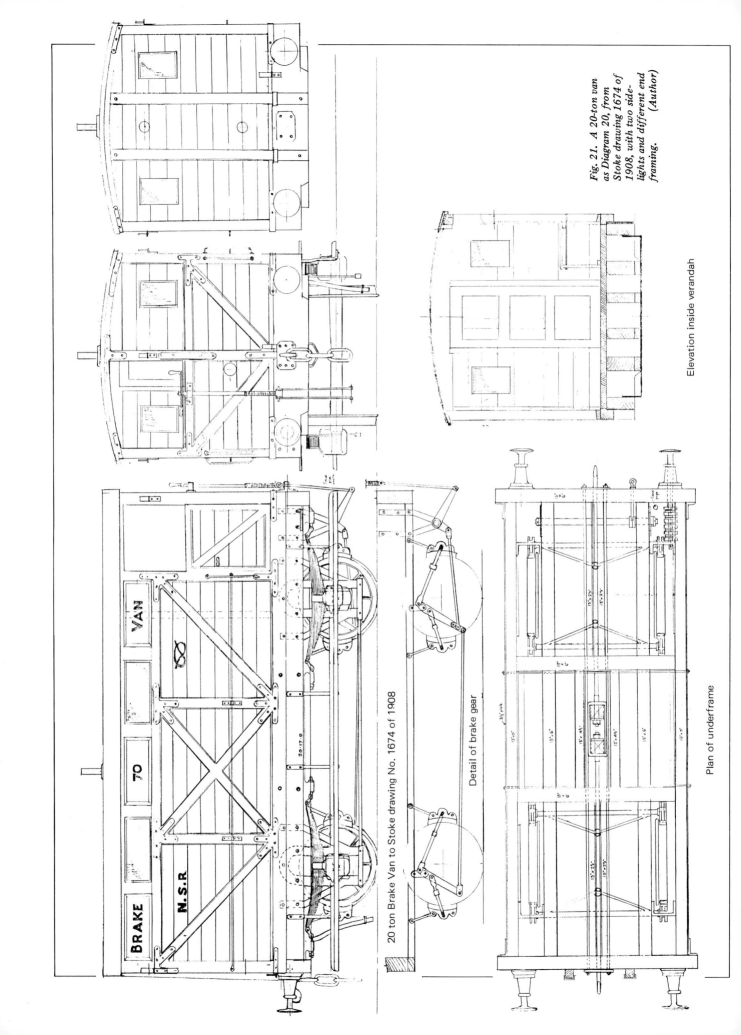

BRAKE 70 VAN N.S.R

20 ton Brake Van to Stoke drawing No. 1674 of 1908

Detail of brake gear

Plan of underframe

Elevation inside verandah

Fig. 21. A 20-ton van as Diagram 20, from Stoke drawing 1674 of 1908, with two side-lights and different end framing. (Author)

¼in plate in the first and ⅜in in the second. Moreover, the design of the frame had changed; in 1888, it closely resembled that of an ordinary wagon, but twenty years later it had no less than six main longitudinal members of 13in depth, and two each of 5in, 6in and 4½in width. The headstocks became 6in x 16in (instead of 5in x 12in) timber. The drawgear was simply arranged in 1888, whereas in 1908 both drawbars were taken back to the centre of the van, and housed in a metal casting containing the springs. The buffing arrangement was also changed, the later van having shorter rods fixed between the solebar, and an iron channel section located above the outer brake shoes, with the spring cylinder attached to the outer face of the channel; the earlier design had the cylinders located near to the centre of the van.

The brake gear was also changed, although the familiar outside handle and vertical screw was retained; seemingly, the NSR felt that the guard or brakesman should be as close as possible to events outside his van, and should be visible from the lineside when applying the brake. The 1888 brake arrangement could be likened to that of a conventional wagon, with V-hangers bolted at the centre of the vehicle. These supported a rod to which was attached links, which in turn were connected to the push rods to each of the four cast iron brake blocks, the hanger rod being connected by a lever and rod to a crank fixed below the van's verandah; the crank was actuated by the external vertical screw and handle. The result, though a little more complicated, was much like that of a wagon hand braking system, except for the position and method of applying the brake, and the greater length of linkage. In the 1908 version, the matter had been re-thought, and the analogy was more with a carriage braking system to some extent. Drawing 1674 shows two brake shoes to each wheel, like a carriage clasp brake. The central V-hangers had been dispensed with, and a much smaller V-bracket took the place of the previous bracket holding the crank, near the end of the van; further, the crank now actuated a linkage of push rods to each wheel, the brake shoes being carried on transverse spindles centrally supported from above. These differing arrangements can be seen most clearly in the view of No. 60 in 1874, and in the G. H. Swann drawing of No. 5421. But it is possible that an intermediate stage in this respect was represented by 'Break 459' at Derby c.1890. This van had a heavy tiebar between the axle guards, seemingly with a single vertical hanger at its midpoint, supporting a possible central axle for the pushrods and corresponding to the previous V-hangers; no other details of 459's brake gear can be made out. It is possible also to interpret a view of No. 2083 (whose body detailing is identical to that of 459) as showing a central vertical hanger; other detail, apart from one set of brake shoes, is obscured. No. 2083, incidentally, shows a variation in the lettering: as a two side-lights van, it has 'BRAKE' on the left end panel and '2083' on the

Plate 23. A 10-ton NSR brake van pictured at Willesden Junction, LNWR, showing the verandah arrangement. *R. J. Essery*

right end panel, with nothing appearing on the central panel between the lights.

Other differences between 1888 and 1908 designs included the reversal of the 'apex upwards' arrangement of end diagonal struts on the later vehicles against that shown on the earlier drawing. The print of drawing No. 1674 shows that they had originally been drawn in the former position, erased, then redrawn to the 'apex downwards' position. Perhaps this was done to enable vans of different tonnage to be identified readily, or maybe there was now a structural justification? The 1908 van was a two side-light design, and had more and heavier strapping to the joints of the outside framework. Two 5⅜in diameter lamp holes were shown on the non-verandah end of the 1908 van, placed centrally one above the other, with one similar hole appearing nearly centrally on the verandah end elevation. The exact purpose of these holes is open to speculation. One theory is that they would be used to show the correct headcodes when trains were being pushed, rather than pulled, a circumstance envisaged by the company's rules in only very few cases. Another view is that they were for exhibiting different lamp codes when running on multiple tracks. At any rate, Brake No. 60 seems to have had them, even if drawing No.68 does not show them at all. No stoves or chimneys are shown on either drawing – were these left to 'local arrangement'?

Vans of 10-ton loading (but of a similar appearance to the 20-ton van) are known, however, so that at least three varieties of goods brake van were in use on the North Stafford during the 1890s and 1990s. It is possible, too, that the earlier, lighter vans may have been upgraded by the addition of heavier frame members and ironwork. The detail differences are well illustrated by the photographed juxtaposition of NSR Nos. 459 and 2091 at Derby, c.1890. No. 2091 appears to be a nominally 10-ton van

Plate 24. A rake of NSR cattle vans at Market Drayton, c.1900–1910. No.5186 shows the Longbottom cattle wagon lettering style well, though the underframe details are masked by the horse, but the tare (6.5.3) and part of the painted number on the solebar can be seen. Both 5186 and its neighbour are lettered '15 FT 10 IN INSIDE', whereas the prototype 5180 is only 15ft 6in inside; it is not known where the extra four inches came from. The whitewashed interiors are clearly visible. These vans had V-hanger brakes one side only, through train pipes, screw couplings, later pattern spring buffers, and grease axleboxes. The NSR 2-plank wagon at the left is of interest in having a 5-link coupling and the webbed pattern of spring buffers used by Longbottom (probably) prior to 1890; it also has the single lever brake.

Shrewsbury Local Studies Library

with one sidelight, and basically looking quite like No. 60 of 1874, except for a continuous footboard and side handrail; the tare weight shown was 9.19.3. Brake No. 459 follows the 1908 drawing two-sidelights arrangement, and has heavier ironwork to the side frames, with the tiebar mentioned above; however, its tare is 10.11.3, i.e. also a nominally 10-ton van. Van No. 2083 has the end strutting 'apex upwards', and has side detailing identical to that of No. 459; its tare seems to be just over 10 tons.

One interesting example of a single-light (probable 10-ton) van was photographed at Crewe North Stafford Junction sometime around 1900. The number of this van can only be guessed at, though it might be 3057. The van is lettered 'BRAKE', and appears to have the heavier sideframe ironwork; it probably has continuous footboards and handrails too. The most interesting feature of the van, though, is that it has the rubber self-contained buffers to be seen on a number of wagons built in the 1860s (e.g. Nos. 2949 and 2995), and also at times on other wagon stock. Many of these latter were converted from dumb-buffers; does this introduce the possibility that some NSR brake vans may have had dumb buffers at earlier times? No doubt the general policy of rebuilding and updating the wagon stock would have applied to brake vans, at least to some extent.

A Typology of NSR Brake Vans

1. Tare unknown, design possibly like J.Wright & Sons L & BR Break, 1849.
2. Tare unknown, no side-lights, details not known; Apedale Break, before 1870?
3. Tare under 10 tons, 1 side light, central V-hanger brake, grease axle boxes, Van No. 60, Gloucester C & W Co., lettered BREAK, 1874.
4. Drawing No. 68, of 1888; Vans 2456 or 2496 (?), and 3057 (?); these with rubber buffers.
5. 10 Ton Van, 1 side-light, centre V-hangers (?), grease boxes; Van No. 2091 and 2074, lettered BREAK, c.1888-1900.
6. 10 Ton Van, 2 side-lights, centre V-hanger, grease boxes; Van No. not known, lettered BRAKE, c.1913.
7. 10 Ton Van, 2 side-lights, single central hanger break, grease boxes, heavy strapping to joints of outside frames; lettered BREAK, Van No. 459, c.1888-1900. Also BRAKE No. 2083.
8. Drawing No. 1674, 2 side-lights, heavier underframe, end V-hanger break, oil axle boxes, 1908.
9. 20 Ton Van, 2 side lights, end V-hanger break, oil boxes, not lettered BRAKE, Van No. 5421 of 1913.

Note: A 20-ton brake van or a van with 2 side-lights seems likely to have been introduced in 1890 or 1891, following the Board of Trade Report on the Accident at Uttoxeter in October 1890. A plan of a 'new goods brake van' was approved by the NSR Finance and Traffic Committee on 2nd December 1890; unfortunately, this plan has not survived.

CATTLE WAGONS

One of the most curious aspects of the NSR minutes is that no reference has been found to the building of cattle wagons or vans during Mr.Longbottom's tenure as Locomotive, Carriage and Wagon Superintendent. The NSR had a stock of 100 cattle wagons in 1870 (and no doubt later), which were then presumably over 20 years old, open to the elements, and apparently fitted with the self-contained or rubber buffers. A view of Ashbourne goods yard c.1880 (Plate 9) shows what appears to be one of these original 'cattle wagons' in a goods train, sheeted over to give some protection to its inhabitants. In 1895, the Board of Agriculture regulations imposed a requirement that cattle 'trucks' should be provided with spring buffers at each end, as well as better footholds. In 1904, these regulations[27] were enlarged to require roofs on all new trucks, means for ventilation and inspection at the floor level, and falling loading doors. The NSR cattle wagons (of 1849/55) were old and greatly out of date, and must have required urgent renewal on modern lines.

Clearly, Mr. Longbottom was responsible for the building of a number of such vehicles, for a photograph of one of his designs was published as part of an illustrated interview with him in March 1901[28]. The vehicle concerned was No. 5180, an 8-ton 'standard' cattle van; it was lettered '15ft 6in Inside', and had a tare of 6.12.0, and may have been similar in some dimensions (but not all) to the 8-ton goods van of 1896. It had the now-standard V-hanger brakes one side only, was fitted with

Plate 25. The *Railway Magazine* (1901) carried an official Stoke photograph of NSR No.5180, a (then) new standard cattle van, roofed and fitted with spring buffers and train pipes; unfortunately, details of the building of these vans have not survived. *Manifold Collection*

through pipe and screw couplings for running in passenger trains, and had the then usual grease, round-based axle boxes provided on Longbottom's wagons.

Subsequently, a number of other vehicles of this general type were built, including Nos. 54, 1685, 1689, 5176, 5183, 5184 (recorded at Weston and Ingestre in 1922), one of them being No. 5186, which was photographed in a rake of at least four similar vehicles at

Market Drayton some time circa 1910[29]. However, there is a slight mystery here, too, for No. 5186 was lettered '15ft 10in Inside', and had a tare weight weight of 6.5.3; another van in the same rake also has this lettering, though its number is obscured. Was the added length contrived by lengthening the whole vehicle? Diagram 10 of the Wagon Diagram Book gives the dimensions of a 6.17.1 tare cattle truck as 16ft 0in over body and 9ft 6in wheelbase which suggests the 15ft 6in internal dimension, not the larger version. No. 5186 and its compatriots at Market Drayton seem to be the same design as 5180, whatever their exact dimensions, and the numbering would suggest a batch of such wagons being all built at once, possibly with No. 5180 as a sample prototype? One possibility is that these vans were constructed in 1896-7, when Longbottom was building new goods vans at Stoke. It will be recalled that 100 new goods vans were ordered from the NSR shops in October 1896, to be supplied by October 1897, and 50 sets of wheels were ordered by tender. At the subsequent committee meeting, Mr. Longbottom reported on the impracticability of this

course, and the NSR order was reduced to 50 vans at £95 each, with a further 50 being obtained from the Metropolitan Carriage Company at £99 each, to be delivered in 15 weeks. It may be that either some of the Stoke fifty were turned out as cattle vans of similar dimensions, or that a small batch was added to this order for goods vans. Certainly, the North Stafford must have been in dire need of some up-to-date vehicles for moving livestock by this time.

It may be that No. 5180 and its companions had a precursor in an *unroofed* version of the same design. A roofless cattle wagon appears in a post-1912 view of Uttoxeter goods yard (Plate 1), and is identical to 5180 except for the absence of a roof, having spring buffers, etc. The tops of the corner posts project above the sides, as in the 1855 Wright design; this suggests a vehicle conceived without a roof, rather than a 5180 type whose roof had been removed, thus dating it between 1895 and 1904. As seen at Uttoxeter, it could not still be employed in the conveyance of livestock, but might well be in use for ale cask traffic.

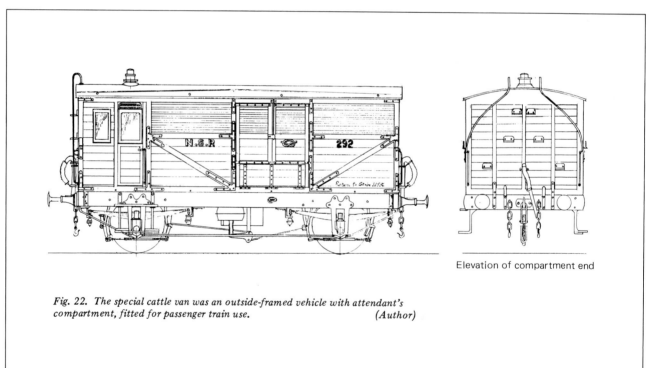

Elevation of compartment end

Fig. 22. The special cattle van was an outside-framed vehicle with attendant's compartment, fitted for passenger train use.   *(Author)*

CHAPTER SEVEN

J.H.ADAMS AND THE NSR AT ITS ZENITH: 1902-1915

JOHN Henry Adams was appointed the Locomotive, Carriage and Wagon Superintendent of the North Staffordshire Railway in March 1902, after the death of Luke Longbottom. John was a son of William Adams (of the Great Eastern, and London and South Western Railways), and had been pupil to his father, learning his profession in a practical manner in the shops, and by having a period on the footplate. Subsequently, he worked in Brazil for 11 years as Locomotive, Carriage and Wagon Superintendent of the Dona Thereza Christina Railway, and afterwards, in January 1899, became Assistant Manager of the SECR Works at Ashford.

One of Adams's first duties on the NSR was to inspect the rolling stock and other plant which the Mersey Railway had for sale in January 1903, but it was found to be unsuitable. Whilst the new Locomotive Superintendent was to make his mark in North Stafford locomotive design by providing a range of appropriate and handsome designs well suited to the needs of the line in the new century, the provision of rolling stock was also demanding attention. Thus, in 1903, two new covered carriage trucks were ordered from the Stoke Shops at £235 each, one in January and one in July. In 1904, it was recorded that 407 out of the company's 6,407 wagons were fitted with either-side brakes, two of which were recorded by the RCH photographically, as already noted. It was ordered that all new wagons (and wagons rebuilt) should in future be fitted with 'independent brake on each side, the same as the L & NW Railway'.

In February 1905, thirty 15-ton limestone wagons were ordered from Stoke – a new design, it would seem.* In May of that year, it was decided that all future rebuilt wagons should be of 15-ton loading. From June to November, a rather protracted negotiation took place with Mr. Cornforth regarding the purchase of 50 second-hand ballast wagons at £20 each, payment being made in old rails, and it was reported in November 'that these wagons had taken the place of others broken up, and had so been numbered. Decided to charge them to Revenue, and also that 25 new 10-ton wagons be built within 12 months on Revenue a/c'.

On 28th November 1905, 12 more new milk vans were ordered, 'large Vans holding 40 Churns each', at £250 each, with '40 Pairs Wheels & Axles @ £17 15s 0d per pair to be ordered by the Secretary from the Leeds Wheel & Axle Co; this cost is included in the above estimate'. The capacity of '40 churns each', when compared with the 1896 6-wheeled type, suggests a 4-wheel van only, though the cost per van (at £250, instead of £190) seems high. Was this an order for 22 or 25ft vans, rather than 20ft?[30]

In May 1906, Mr. Adams apparently suggested a change in the colour of NSR wagons, no doubt in line with his changes in engine and carriage livery; however, what the colour was to be, or the outcome of the subsequent experiment do not seem to be recorded.

Six 'duplicate' open carriage trucks were ordered from the shops in June at a cost of £158 18s 0d on Revenue account; these were Nos. 2-7.

*To Diagram 16, 17ft 6in x 7ft 0in with 5ft 6in sides.

Plate 26. NSR 10-ton wagon No.6103 was built by the Metropolitan C & W Co. in 1902 (tare 6.1.3), and is pictured at Edge Hill on 26th April 1904, fitted with the NS 'either-side' brake. The wagon has only one pair of brake shoes, despite having a handle each side. Although approved by the Board of Trade, this brake does not seem to have been other than experimental, and the usual V-hanger arrangement became the NSR standard, although at first being fitted to one side of each wagon. *Public Record Office*

Plate 27. Three-plank, 10-ton open No.1880, with internal strapping.

Manifold Collection

Plates 28 & 29. Variations in the form of the Staffordshire knot and the placing of the NSR numberplate are shown in these examples of 3-plank wagons with the later oil axleboxes.   R. J. Essery

Plate 30. Ex-NSR 3-plank 10-ton wagon No.193309 in LMS service. The vehicle had oil axleboxes and internal strapping, with a tare weight of 5.0.2. No.193309 was fitted with plain buffer castings and V-hanger brakes. Note the headstock repair. *G. H. Platt*

On 19th March 1907, The Directors Minute Book No. 5[31] recorded:

Carriages and Passenger Vans:
1. 190 Small 4 wheel stock to be gradually replaced out of Revenue by large stock.
2. Running stock = 280.
   8 New carriages and 4 Passenger Vans to be added out of Revenue as depreciation every year.
3. Duplicate stock to be increased every year by deplaced Running Stock.
4. Carriages to be brought up to 80 Passenger standard.

Wagons, etc = 6,407 Running stock
1. 200 new Wagons to be built each year out of Revenue.
2. Duplicate stock = 63; to be increased each year by deplaced Running Stock, which need not be broken up at once.
Shop extensions & extra Machinery as necessary'.

This policy was confirmed.

1907 also showed modest additional wagon activity. Two second-hand tip wagons were bought in March of that year, whilst six new brake vans at £190 each, and twenty-five 15-ton coal wagons at £93 each were ordered from the company's shops in June. In October, the Traffic Committee replied to a letter from the Board of Trade concerning the derailment in July of NSR wagon No. 2995 at Waleswood (on the Great Central), to the effect that: 'such wagons are reconstructed on modern lines when brought into the Shops for repairs, or as opportunity occurs'. A quiet period then ensued, with only 12 new narrow-gauge tipping wagons for Caldon New Quarry (at £15 each) being recorded in 1908. However, in 1910 activity began again. Six new (open) carriage trucks were ordered in July, to an approved plan (vehicles Nos. 8-13), and in October Mr. Adams was instructed: 'to bring up Tenders for building 25 New Locomotive Coal Wagons at the next Meeting. He was reminded that the Directors had already authorised his working full time in the Wagon

Shops', − an indication that things had been a little slack there, for some time. Cravens Ltd. subsequently built these loco coal wagons at £91 15s 0d each. Seven milk vans (Nos. 295, 297-300, 305 and 320) were also built in 1910.

Replacement of Old Wagons, 1909-1914

Year	Replaced	By	
1909 (second half)	63 6-ton wagons	9	8-ton wagons
		29	10-ton "
		25	15-ton "
1910 (first half)	58 6-ton wagons	9	8-ton wagons
		49	10-ton "
1911 (second half)	98 6-ton goods and mineral wagons	19	8-ton wagons
		54	10-ton "
		25	15-ton "
1912 (second half)	72 6-ton open wagons	4	8-ton open wagons
		66	10-ton " "
1913 (first half)	149 6-ton wagons	155	10-ton wagons
	9 8-ton "	3	15-ton "
1914 (second half)	185 wagons (and 19 carriages)		

Source: *Railway and Travel Monthly*

Six new 6-wheel milk vans, at an estimated cost of £268 each, were then put out to tender in November, but the successful bid, by the Metropolitan Amalgamated Railway Carriage & Wagon Co. in January 1911, was at £325 each, 'with their own wheels'. The Metropolitan Co. milk vans were numbered 174-179, 179 being photographed at Saltley. Nos. 302 & 322 are also recorded in 1911, presumably built at Stoke. Also in 1911, Cravens tendered successfully for twenty five 30ft, 15-ton, 6-wheeled rail or timber trucks − a new design, though one seemingly unrecorded by any drawing, diagram, or photograph, although drawings exist for a 4-wheeled version (Stoke No. 1785 of 2/4/11) of 10ft wheelbase, and also one on a 20ft wheelbase (drawing No. 1846 of 1/10/12, Diagram 19).

Fig. 23. Ex-NSR 3-plank 10-ton wagon with oil axleboxes and external diagonal strapping. (National Railway Museum)

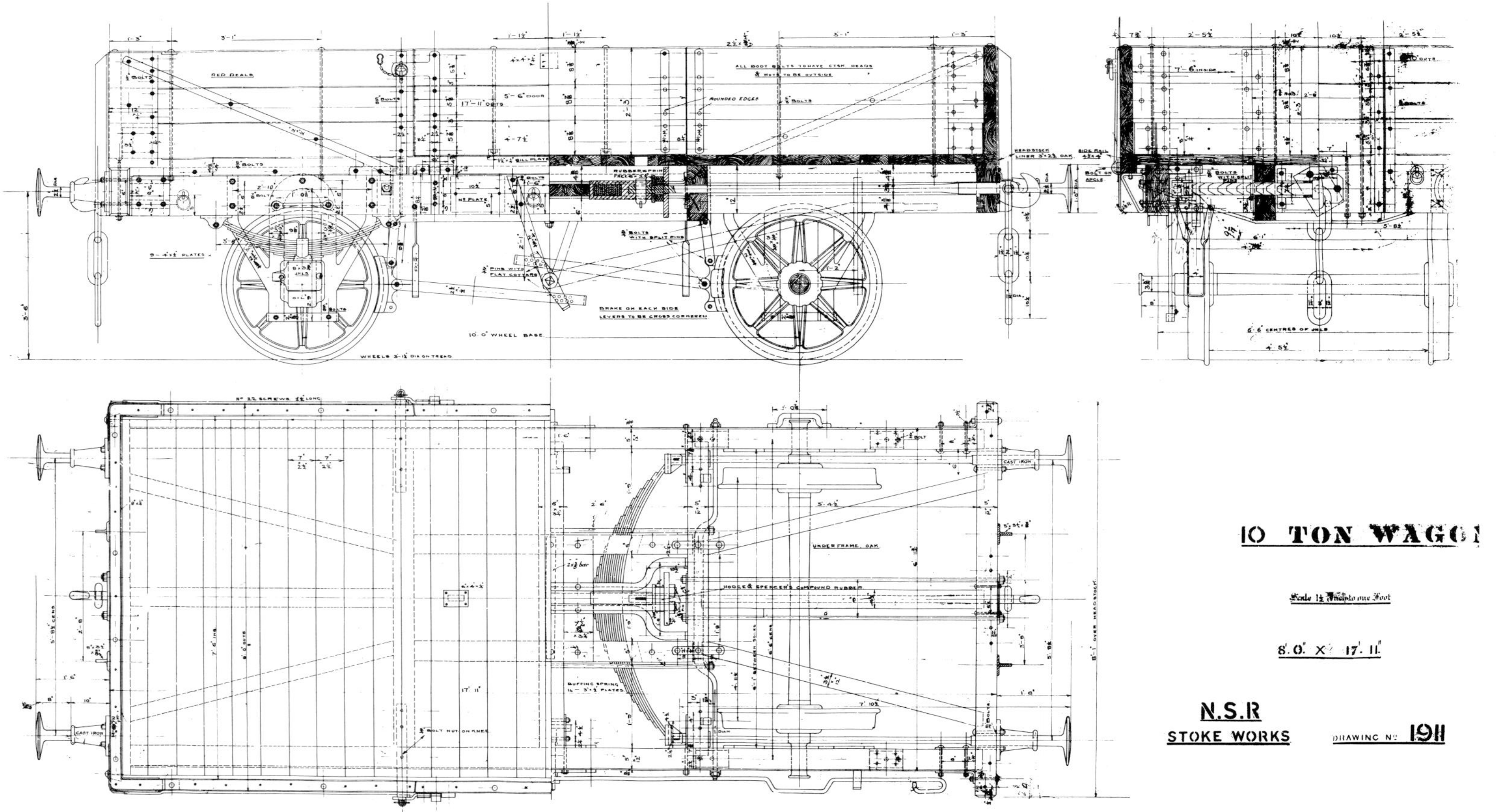

IO TON WAGON

Scale 1½ Inches one Foot

8' 0" × 2' 17' 11"

N.S.R

STOKE WORKS

DRAWING Nº 1911

Plates 31 & 32. No.4051 and No.01113, fitted with oil axleboxes and external diagonal strapping.
R. J. Essery & J. R. Hollick

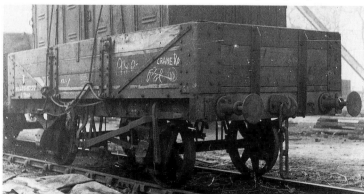

Plate 33. Three-plank, 10-ton open, LMS No.197177 pictured at Renfrew on 10th March 1946. The vehicle was built at Stoke in 1920.
A. G. Ellis / R. J. Essery. Collection

Plate 34. Another ex-NSR 3-plank vehicle in LMS service. No.196681 has grease axleboxes and external strapping.
R. Pochin

Plate 34a. The second vehicle in this Up Belfast Boat Express of 1899 appears to be an NSR 22ft Milk Van with end louvres, and outward opening doors.

Plate 35. There were at least two varieties of 4-wheel milk vans built between 1889 and 1895, with 7- or 8-plank sides; the diagram book shows a 7-plank version with the band of louvres continued around the ends, but no photograph has been found of one with this feature. The goods and milk train leaving Tutbury has, as the first vehicle, a 4-wheel, 7-plank van with in-set doors, followed by a similar 6-wheeler; then there is a 4-wheel type with outside doors, and 4-wheelers, probably with inset doors; all are of the 'narrow band of louvres' design.

Author's Collection

SECTION THRO FRAMING

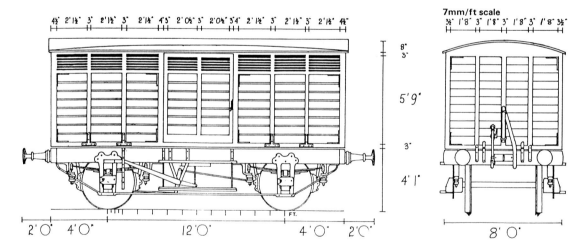

Fig. 24. This drawing is of an 8-plank van and is based on measurements of a grounded body; in its original condition, though, it would have had grease, not oil, axleboxes.   (T. W. Bourne)

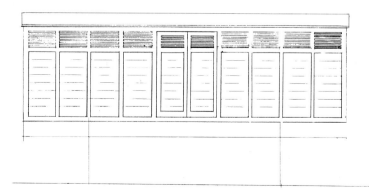

Fig. 25. Another 8-plank milk van, 22ft in length.   (Author)

NSR Milk Van built by the Metropolitan Carriage & Wagon Co. in 1911.

G. Dow Collection

Plate 36. Six-wheel milk vans were built in two main types, with shallow or deep bands of louvres; however, the shallow louvre type also existed in both 7- and 8-plank versions, and the deep louvres type had either inset or outside sliding doors. The photograph shows an 8-plank 6-wheeler at Froghall. *National Railway Museum*

Plate 37. Ex-NSR 6-wheel van with inset doors, M38672M at Crow Road Sidings, Glasgow, September 1956, still with NSR 1914 builder's plate.
F. W. Shuttleworth

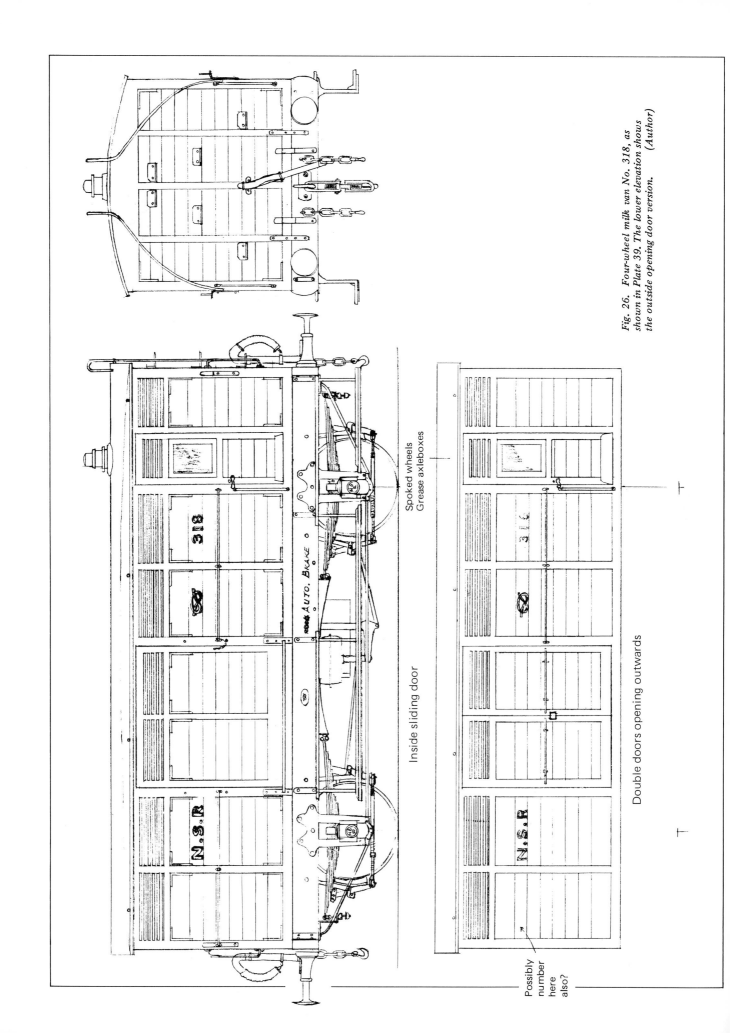

Spoked wheels
Grease axleboxes

Inside sliding door

Double doors opening outwards

Possibly number here also?

Fig. 26. Four-wheel milk van No. 318, as shown in Plate 39. The lower elevation shows the outside opening door version. (Author)

Plate 38. Some milk vans were conversions from older carriages; some 35ft 6in stock was converted during the Great War for aeroplane traffic. An LNWR milk train, headed by 4-4-0 No.1978 *Merlin*, conveys such a vehicle in post-WW1 days; the first vehicle is an aeroplane/milk van, followed by two NSR milk vans of the earlier, 6-wheel design. *L&GRP, cty. David & Charles*

Then, in July 1911, Harrison & Camm of Rotherham successfully tendered for 6 new silk vans at £224 15s 0d each, to drawing No. 1790 of 13th June 1911. Whether silk vans, as special vehicles, had been provided previously is not clear; ordinary goods vans may have been used for this traffic, which had been carried for some time between Macclesfield, Congleton, Leek and London, by various routes. These vans were listed as goods stock, but were fitted with carriage wheels, screw couplings, and the vacuum brake; tare was 8.1.0, but numbers allocated are not known. No photograph of these vehicles has yet been found.

In October 1911, it was minuted that 6 goods brake vans were required, their usual price being £260 each; however, the successful tender went out to Cravens, at £315 each, their design being very similar to that of

Plate 39. Milk van No.318, pictured at Tutbury milk dock c.1890-1906. This was formerly a fatstock van, hence the attendant's compartment. *L&GRP, cty. David & Charles*

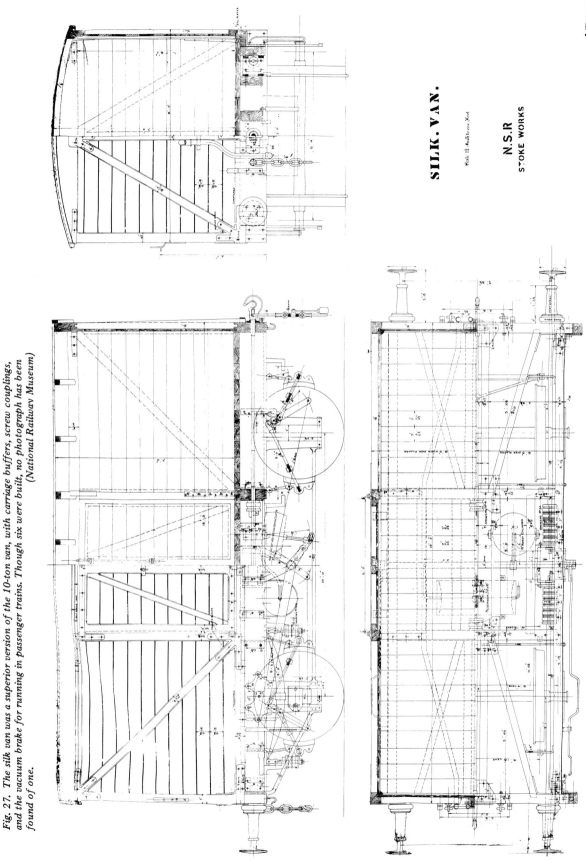

Fig. 27. The silk van was a superior version of the 10-ton van, with carriage buffers, screw couplings, and the vacuum brake for running in passenger trains. Though six were built, no photograph has been found of one.
(National Railway Museum)

SILK. VAN.

N.S.R
STOKE WORKS

DRAWING Nº 1790

drawing No. 1674 of 1908. Brake No. 5421 was one of the batch to be delivered, and a photograph of it (when new) survives.

In November, tenders for fifty 10-ton new goods vans were called for, the bid of the Metropolitan Amalgamated Railway Carriage & Wagon Co. being accepted (at £128 each), with delivery in 16 weeks. Drawing No. 1812 of 25th November 1911 illustrates these vehicles.

'40 duplicate wagons for replacement' were ordered in February 1912, with no other details given. Under the heading of 'Wagons Off for Repairs' in May, Mr. Adams was authorised to invite tenders for 50 new 10-ton wagons, in which the Birmingham C & W Co. was successful at £105 15s 0d each. In September, a further 25 (10-ton) wagons were approved from the same source, but this time at £112 5s 0d each. Twelve new horse boxes 'to the plan submitted by Loc. Supt.' were ordered to be built

Plate 40. Goods van No.5511, built c.1896, seen on a Manifold Valley transporter car, c.1908; it has V-hanger brakes one side only.
J. W. Walker

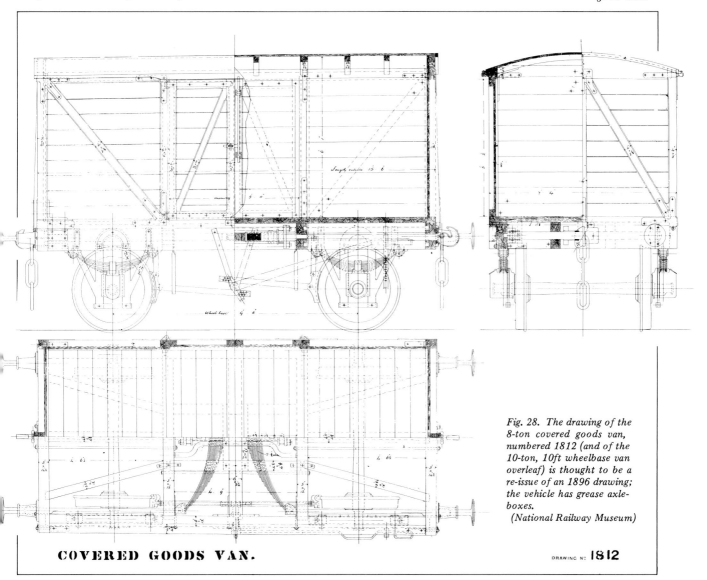

COVERED GOODS VAN.

Fig. 28. The drawing of the 8-ton covered goods van, numbered 1812 (and of the 10-ton, 10ft wheelbase van overleaf) is thought to be a re-issue of an 1896 drawing; the vehicle has grease axle-boxes.
(National Railway Museum)

DRAWING N° 1812

COVERED GOODS
WAGON.

N.S.R
STOKE WORKS

DRAWING N.º 1812

Fig. 29. The covered goods van drawing of 1911, also numbered 1812, is of the 10-ton,
10ft wheelbase van with oil axleboxes.
(National Railway Museum)

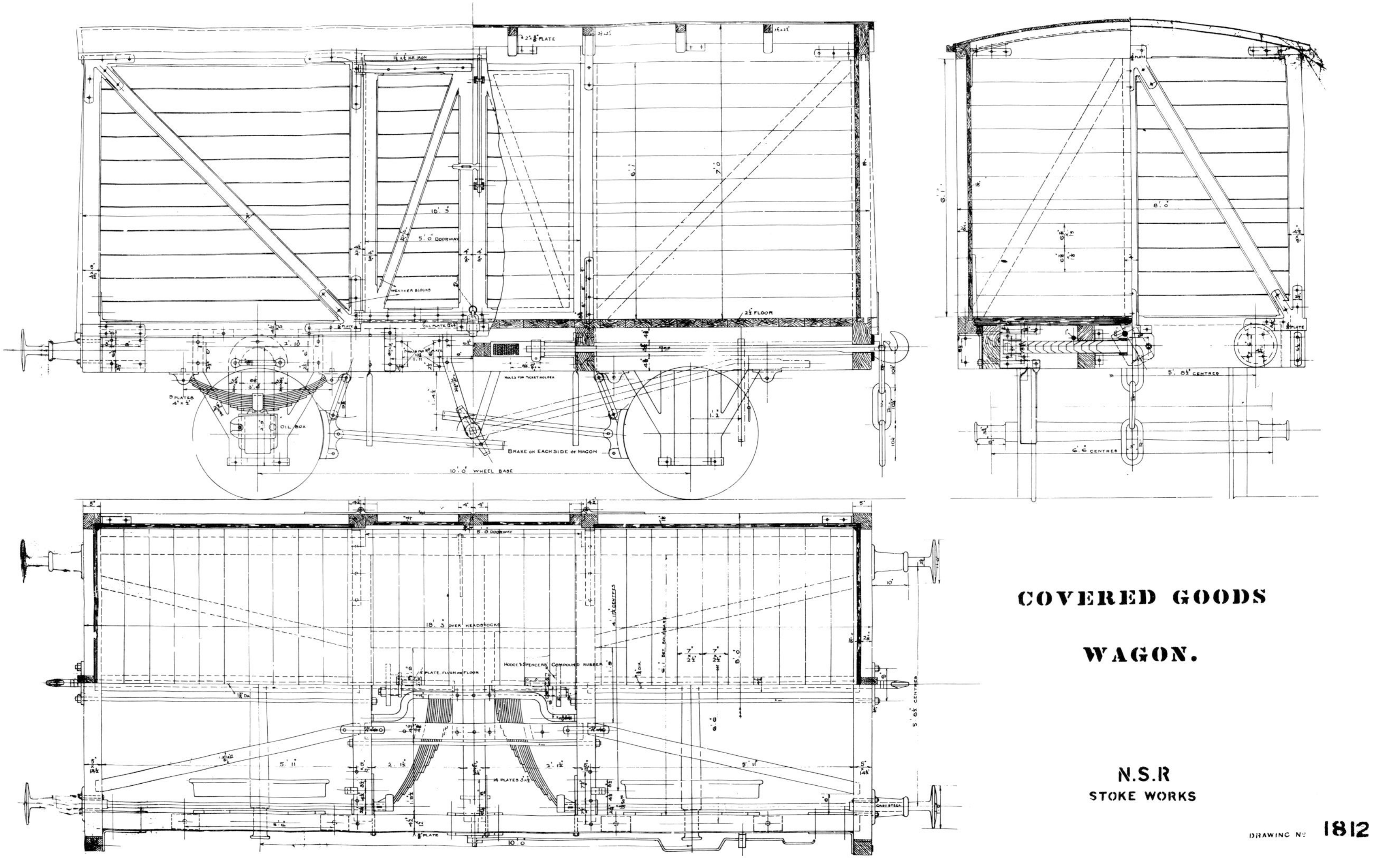

Plate 41. 10-ton NSR covered goods No.5489.
R. J. Essery

Plate 42. An official view of 10-ton NSR van No.5427, built by the Metropolitan RC & W Company in 1912 as one of a batch of fifty to Order
No.B1771. Note the position of the knot on these vans.   *Birmingham City Libraries*

in the company's shops at £280 each in October 1912. The 'plan' in question would appear to be the copy drawings Nos. 1946/47; seemingly, these were a re-issue and updating of the 1898 design, as grease axle boxes are shown, although the later semi-elliptical roof profile was adopted. In November 1912, 50 new 10-ton wagons, at £117 5s 0d each, were ordered from Cravens. It seems that the Committee's determination to have 15-ton wagons had not been entirely a firm one.

One milk van was added in each of the years 1912 and 1913 (Nos. 303 and 304 respectively), and four more, Nos. 318, 321, 323 & 330, were built in 1914. Three more, probably 6-wheel, were built in 1916, and one in 1917: Nos. 319, 324, 331 and 325.

In July 1913, it was stated that a 'New Travelling Crane' was required for traffic purposes, at a cost of £324; the relevant minute sturdily asserted: 'Standardise and make for ourselves'. Following this, in December, the Stores Committee's recommendations were approved for 50 trucks, under a heading 'Dead-buffered wagons: the rest to be adapted as soon as possible'. No doubt this was a reference to the RCH ruling on the cessation of use of dumb-buffered wagons, except as departmental stock, after 1913.

On 6th October 1914, shortly after the outbreak of the Great War, an order was reported for '42 General Service Wagons to be built for the Artillery Section of the War Office'.

On 9th February 1915, the minutes refer to 'Insanitary Milk Vans. As the Vans come in for general repairs to be fitted with Decolite flooring at a cost of £10 0s 0d per Van, £3 3s 0d per Van being saved in wood required. Total number of Vans 89'.

John Adams died suddenly in December 1915.

Plate 43. Ex-NSR 10-ton van No.196734, seen in LMS service, with brakes both sides, but changed axleboxes.   *R. J. Essery*

CHAPTER EIGHT

THE FINAL YEARS OF THE NORTH STAFFORD

WARTIME conditions did not allow much new wagon building, except for war purposes; however, there are several items of interest to be found in the minutes:

'**27th June 1916:** Wagons – To cease building for a time. Men can work in Smithy on Munitions as far as possible. 110 6-ton wagons to be scrapped, and 10-ton wagons in lieu thereof to be built on conclusion of War. Replace the 17 (16 6-ton & 1 8-ton). *(The latter comment is a little cryptic! – Author)*
'**19th September 1916:** 15 Ton Rail Trucks – 25 of these to be built in substitution of 50 of the old 6-ton trucks ordered to be broken up. Plan approved at an estimated cost of £296 each. Cost of rebuilding 2 of the 6-tonners estimated at £270. Tenders for Wheels & Axles, Timber, etc., to be obtained.
'**28th November 1916:** Railway Wagons for use Overseas – At the request of the Executive Committee 25 wagons to be built in the Company's Shops.
'**12th June 1917:** Combined Passenger & Brake Coach for Woolwich Arsenal – Reported sold for £65. Approved
Locomotives for Overseas – General Manager's reply approved. (6 Engines put by for the Government not yet taken)'.

Subsequently, in January 1918, 12 six-ton wagons were to be sold to the Admiralty 'at £25 each on rail at Stoke'.

In May 1918, under the heading 'Covered Vehicles for Conveyance of Aeroplanes', it was reported that the Government 'had commandeered 21 Third class Brakes used as milk vans to be converted to 35 feet. Old Third class carriages to be used for carrying milk.' Later, at the same meeting, it was minuted '10 of the 35ft vehicles to be converted'. Thus, it seems that two batches of old 6-wheel carriages were under discussion: 21 old Third Brakes already in use as milk vans, and now to be converted for aeroplane traffic for the Government, and 10 Third class carriages (not Brakes) to be converted to milk use by the company in place of the first 21 (the 21 were part of 31 passenger vehicles which had 'disappeared' in 1915/16, 8 of them being sent to France, the others being non-passenger carrying vehicles). From mid-1917, the Government had been commandeering theatrical scenery trucks and other suitable vans to carry partly assembled aeroplanes[32], and it appears that even the NSR's old milk vans were usable for this purpose. The NSR apparently modified the additional 10 carriages, but at the end of the war re-converted those 10 aeroplane vans for milk use again, as a minute of 26th November 1918 records. It seems that these 10 vans never left the NSR, and they survived in traffic even after the Grouping, and were recorded as Diagram 10 in the NSR Non-Passenger Carrying Coaching Stock Diagrams.

Later in 1918, it was recorded that the last of the twenty-five 15-ton rail trucks ordered in September 1916 had been turned out.

With the war over, and J.A.Hookham installed as the new Locomotive Engineer (from 1916), a 'taking stock of

the situation' was indicated. On 18th February 1919, the Locomotive Engineer presented his report on the carriage and wagon stock at the end of 1918, and a proposed building programme for 1919. The wagon stock then consisted of 6,097 vehicles, and replacement of old 6-ton wagons by 10-ton vehicles was proceeding apace. It was hoped to build 200 new wagons during 1919, at a cost of £220 each.

In April 1919, two 12-ton implement wagons were ordered (at £400 each) as replacements of two existing wagons; these were Nos. 771 and 3484, each of tare 7.18.0, and represented by Diagram 21. From the survival of several drawings of such wagons designed by the Midland Railway in the NRM collection of Stoke drawings, it seems likely that the NSR wagons owed something to their larger neighbours at Derby.

In February 1920, it was reported that 150 wagons was to be the limit for that year's building programme at Stoke, with possibly 200 in the next year. Tenders were to be obtained for 200 wagons from outside firms, whilst 200 wagons were already on order from the Ince Wagon Co.

In March 1920, 376 additional wagons were contemplated, this figure being raised to 576 in May: 'Tenders to be obtained for 50 12-ton trucks and the remainder 10-ton trucks. 50 Twin Bolster and 50 10-ton trucks to be built in the Company's Shops.' In June, the intention was modified to the purchase of fifty 12-ton wagons only, apart from the Stoke order, which remained unaltered. In March 1921, a further fifty 10-ton wagons (total cost £15,000) were deleted from the building programme.

More milk vans then followed: '7th December 1920: new Milk vans required. Six to be built at an estimated cost of £1,115 each in March, but subject to enquiry as to new designs.' It is not clear whether these vans were to be tendered for, or built at Stoke. It was also reported that the offer by the Government of the loan of ten 20-ton goods brake vans should be accepted, although the origin of these war surplus vehicles is not known.

Ten further milk vans were added to stock in 1921; Nos. 60, 92, 262, 265, 266, 270, 326, 365, 366 & 372.

What seems to be the last minuted reference to ordinary NSR wagons occurred on 19th July 1921, when some twenty-five 8-ton wagons were ordered to be rebuilt into 10-ton vehicles at an estimated cost of £200 each. It was also reported that stores van No. 597 had been destroyed by fire at Mow Cop two weeks earlier.

The year 1921 also saw the advent of the two largest types of wagon ever owned by the North Stafford:

'1st March 1921. Special Vehicles – The Tender of the Metropolitan Carriage & Wagon Company was accepted for Two 25-ton Well Trucks – 52ft 11in long over headstocks at a cost of £2,897 each, and two 30-ton Trollies 41ft 0in over headstocks at

Plate 44. A rake of NSR coal wagons at Crewe North Stafford Sidings, including an iron wagon (left) which seems to be marked 'LOCO ... COAL'. Also in view are a 5-plank, a 3- or 4-plank, and another 5-plank; all are dumb-buffered.

J. P. Richards

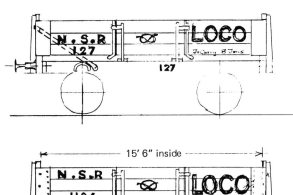

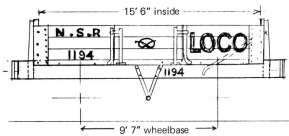

Figs. 30, 31 & 32. The drawings on this page are of 6-ton, 3-plank wagons Nos. 127 and 1194, and 10-ton, 5-plank No. 5261, the latter pair with V-hanger brakes one side only and 5-link couplings, and all as running c.1895. No. 127 (Fig. 30) was equipped with spring buffers, grease axleboxes (round-base), brakes one side only (probably single-lever), and inside diagonal strapping. Wagon No. 1194 had dumb buffers, flat-based axle-boxes and internal diagonal strapping (Fig. 31). As in the case of the foregoing, the drawing of No. 5261 (Fig. 32) was constructed from a photograph of several wagons at Podmore Hall Colliery; the livery — red oxide body, black ironwork and white lettering. (Author)

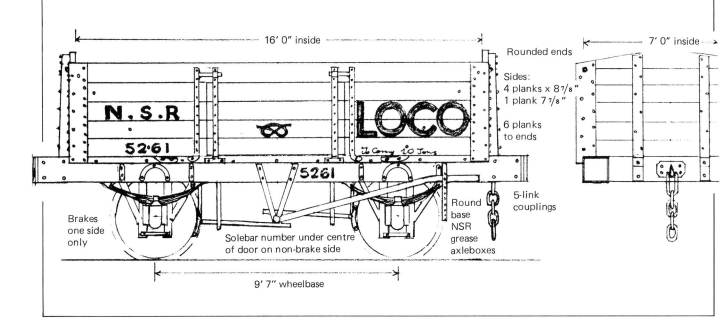

£2,150 each. Total cost £10,094 to be charged to Revenue, instead of building 33 10-ton Wagons (part of the 50 wagons to be built on Revenue) given in programme as the Trucks and Trollies are urgently required.'

Appropriately, in view of the long association between the two companies, the last order went to the same firm which, under another name, had supplied some of the first rolling stock for the railway, although these final wagons were to be built at Wednesbury, rather than Saltley.

At the Grouping of the railway companies, the NSR became part of the London, Midland & Scottish Railway, and its rolling stock became absorbed into a greater mass of vehicles. Non-standard types of wagons did not last too long in this new environment and, apart from a few open wagons, little photographic evidence of North Stafford rolling stock has survived.

The North Stafford goods livery seems to have been more or less constant throughout the company's history, and like that of several other concerns, was based upon red oxide. However, descriptions of the exact shade used vary from dark red-brown* to purplish red oxide; solebars, headstocks, and corner plates were usually black. Lettering (6 inch to 1912, 14 inch thereafter) was white, originally shaded black; the knot was also white, but had some variation in size and shape.

Non-passenger coaching stock was presumably Victoria brown, changing to madder lake at the same time as carriage stock, late in 1903.

LOCOMOTIVE COAL WAGONS

Locomotive coal wagons are an interesting sub-species of ordinary open wagon stock. The earliest NSR open coal wagons, it is surmised, were the wrought-iron bodied type, seen in several of the accompanying illustrations. Wagons of this type were in general use in The Potteries by private owners; for instance, Parkhouse Collieries and Robert Heath & Son used them. Heath's ironworks, in fact, were builders of this type of wagon, as well as users, and the wagons seem to have varied in height. Heath's 10-ton wagon No. 305, lettered 'R H & S', appears on a well-known postcard c.1905-1910 on a Manifold Valley transporter in an L & MVLR train, and looks about 4 planks high side equivalent; the NSR wagons were lower, about 3 planks equivalent. These NSR wagons had wooden underframes and (originally) dumb buffers, converted to spring buffers in some cases, noted by the 1890s; at least one such conversion, wagon No. XX49, had the self-contained rubber buffers. Brakes were of the simple early type, one side only, and axle boxes had the flat base. Some of these iron-bodied wagons are known lettered as for ordinary open wagons. The locomotive coal wagons of this kind invariably had the word 'LOCO' at the *left*-hand end, about mid-height, and the number likewise at the right-hand end.

Of wooden-bodied loco coal wagons, 3, 4, and 5-plank versions have been noted, although possibly a few more of the 5-plank variety appear photographically, though this may be misleading. The 5-plank wagon appears fairly universally with dumb buffers up to 1912 at least, whilst the 3 and 4-plank versions are seen both with dumb buffers and spring buffers. All three types had rounded or higher end planks. These wagons would have had grease axle boxes, probably of the later round-based type, and the early pattern of brake, though one dumb-buffered 5-plank wagon is known with V-hanger brakes, presumably to one side only. All these wooden wagons had the word 'LOCO', about two planks high, at the *right*-hand end, but some variations in its placing are known. On the 5-plank versions, no lettering normally appeared higher than the top of the third plank, i.e. the top of the 'N.S.R.' was level with the top of the 'LOCO' at this height, but on 3 and 4-plank wagons there was some variation in this general relationship. The numbers on these wagons appeared on the bottom plank, below the company's initials, whilst 'To Carry X Tons' was on the bottom plank, below the 'LOCO'; the number was painted on the solebar, below the knot.

It is likely that most loco coal wagons were old stock approaching obsolescence, or were bought second-hand from private owners or wagon builders; there are several entries in the NSR minutes suggestive of this practice. Also, obsolete dumb-buffered stock could enjoy a prolonged life by turning it over to such traffic. However, some loco coal wagons as such were built by the NSR, and in Adams's time, a batch of 7-plank 15-ton wagons were built for this purpose, to Diagram 15, on a 10ft wheelbase. These wagons were 17ft 5in long inside, and had three widths: 7ft, 7ft 2in, and 7ft 6in, with tare weights 7.2.0, 7.5.2, and 7.10.0 respectively; spring buffers, oil axle boxes, and V-hanger brakes both sides were fitted, in accordance with the latest NSR practice. These wagons were probably built from 1905, and thus carried the small lettering style for quite some time. In 1913, a 17ft by 8ft version of this 15-ton, 7-plank wagon (50in side) was built; these ran with the then new, large N (knot) S lettering style from new.

* (like the Caledonian and Highland Railways)

Fig. 33. The Stoke drawing of the 7-plank, 15-ton coal wagon of 1913. (National Railway Museum)

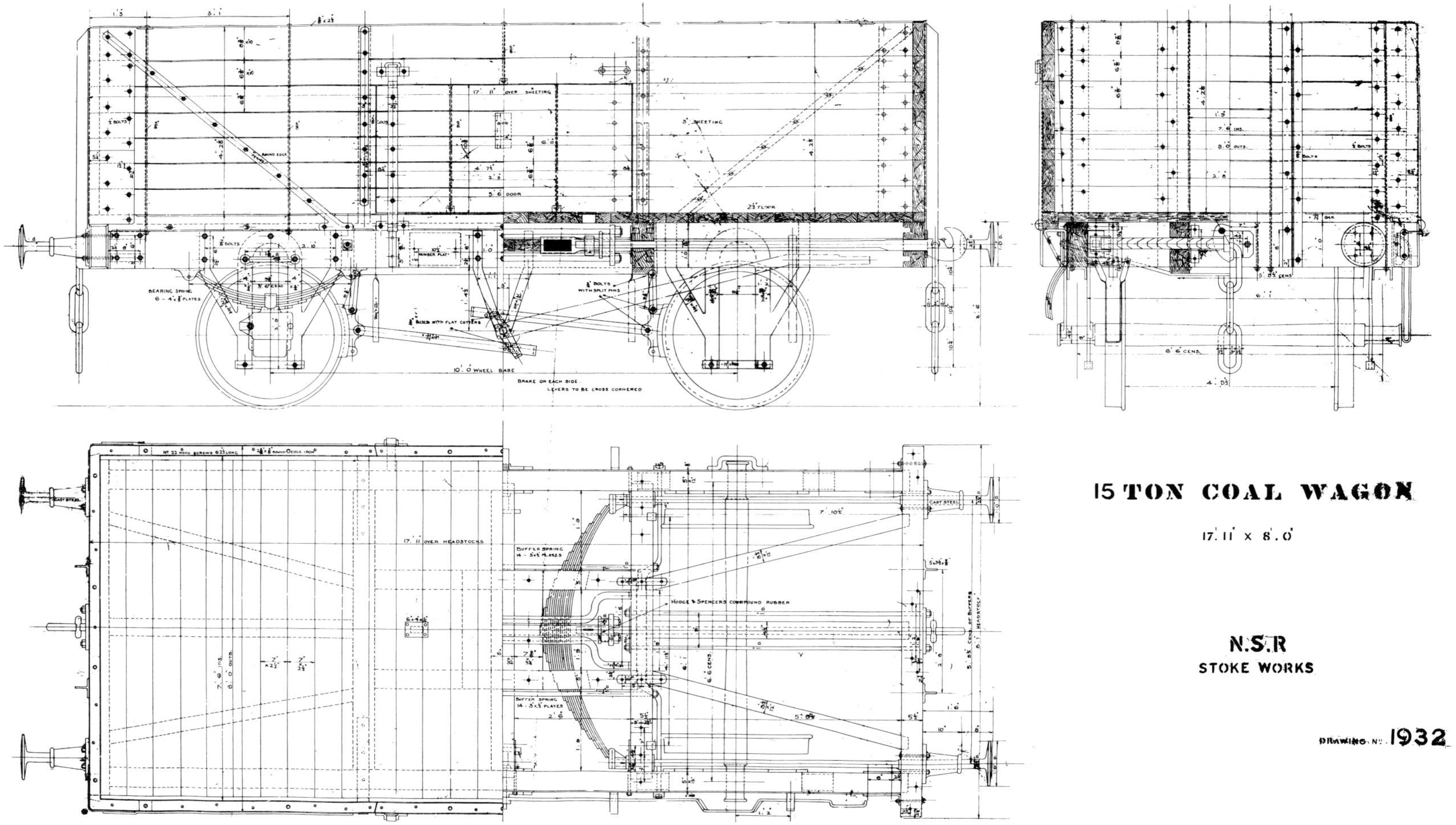

15 TON COAL WAGON

17'.11' × 8'.0'

N.S.R
STOKE WORKS

DRAWING No. 1932

Plate 45. The North Stafford used both iron and wooden loco coal wagons, the former being manufactured locally by the ironmaster Robert Heath; they were of wrought iron on a wooden underframe, with sides 2ft 6in or 3ft high, and 15ft long. Use was also made of second-hand wagons from various sources, including dumb-buffered stock. The photograph of Pratt's Sidings was taken soon after 1885, when engine No.49 was built. The end of an iron loco wagon can be seen at right, it has dumb buffers and old-pattern grease axleboxes. The lettering is of interest – these iron wagons had 'LOCO' at the left end, whereas wooden wagons displayed it at the right end. *Manifold Collection*

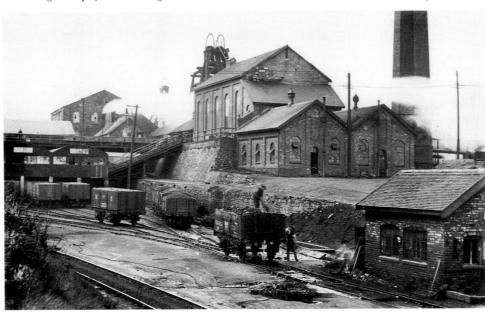

Plate 46. John Adams introduced a new design of 7-plank wagon, mostly for loco coal use; here, at Burley Pit, Apedale, one such vehicle stands in the yard with private owner wagons, and what might possibly be a dumb-buffered NSR loco coal wagon of 4- or 5-plank design. *A. C. Baker*

LIMESTONE OR HOPPER WAGONS

Limestone from the NSR's own quarry at Caldon Low was an important freight commodity on the railway. For a very long time it was carried in ordinary low-sided wagons (as evidenced by photographs of Froghall Wharf, the terminus of the tramway from the quarry via inclined planes to canal and railhead, until the Leek – Waterhouses line was opened in 1904). Subsequently, further provision for the stone traffic was made by the construction of the Endon Tippler, to facilitate rail/canal transfer of this commodity.

Special hopper wagons were built for the limestone traffic, and certainly from 1905, when thirty 15-ton limestone wagons were ordered from Stoke, no doubt with a view to their use on the new Caldon Low branch. Diagram 16 of the later NSR Diagram Book shows a 3-plank hopper wagon with bottom doors and inclined flooring; it was 27in high in the sides, with side doors and rounded ends, and in appearance was a conventional 3-plank wagon. Dimensions were: 17ft 5in inside x 7ft 0in, on a 10ft wheelbase. Its tare was 7.0.0. No constructional drawing has survived of this vehicle, although three examples might be seen in the J. Walker view of a stone train on the Churnet Valley line taken about this period.

Later, in 1912, a 5-plank version was designed at Stoke, having $42\frac{3}{4}$in sides, but with flat tops to the wagon ends; otherwise it was dimensionally similar to the earlier 3-plankers, and still with a 15-ton payload. It is not clear whether any of these wagons were indeed built (like the 1913 version of the cattle wagon, for which a detailed drawing also exists) for no other evidence of their having actually been constructed has been found. Other vehicles which were designed at this time, but which do not appear to have been built, include the 6-wheel rail wagons actually ordered from Cravens (apparently being substituted by the 4-wheel 20ft wheelbase rail wagons), and two timber trucks, one 14ft overall on an 8ft 6in wheelbase, and the other 16ft long on a 9ft 6in wheelbase.

Plate 47. A train of stone from Froghall, working hard along the Churnet Valley. Most of the wagons are 2-plank, though at least two single-plank wagons are visible. Potentially the most interesting wagons, though, are the three 3-plank design; these might possibly be 15-ton hopper wagons to Diagram 16, with bottom and side doors, and rounded ends. They were a Longbottom design, and would have had grease axleboxes and brakes one side only. Most of the wagons in the train are fitted with the single lever brake one side only; all seem to have spring buffers. The period of the photograph is after 1903 and before 1912.

J. W. Walker

Plate 48. A photograph showing the transfer of limestone at Froghall Basin c.1900 from the 3ft 6in gauge to the standard system. Horses were used for shunting, and most of the wagons used were of the 1- or 2-plank design; only one 3-plank wagon can be seen here.

Manifold Collection

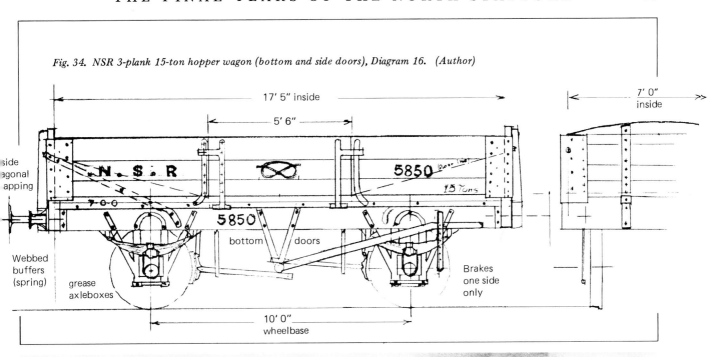

Fig. 34. NSR 3-plank 15-ton hopper wagon (bottom and side doors), Diagram 16. (Author)

Plate 49. Another stone train, seen here leaving Froghall c.1905–1910; the engine is rebuilt Sharp, Stewart No.64. Again, the wagons are predominantly of 2-plank design. Note the 'S' shunt signal.
                                                                                                                            J. W. Walker

Plates 50 & 51.   The Endon Tippler: as the third largest railway owner of canals, the North Staffordshire had a direct interest in fostering traffic on the Caldon Canal, and all this coincided with its ownership of the Caldon Low Quarry. With a large increase in the demand for limestone from Caldon by Brunner Mond of Northwich, the NSR erected a new wagon tippler at Endon (on the Leek Brook–Stoke line) in 1917, thus adding to the existing resources of the Waterhouse branch, the Froghall Incline (which was not closed until 1920), and Froghall Wharf. The tippler was designed and fabricated at Stoke. Some less usual rolling stock is to be seen in addition to wagon No.2221 – a 6-wheel hand crane and a 3-plank wagon fitted with a sheet bar are present, as well as another 3-plank dropside wagon (c.1917).

Manifold Collection

TIMBER WAGONS

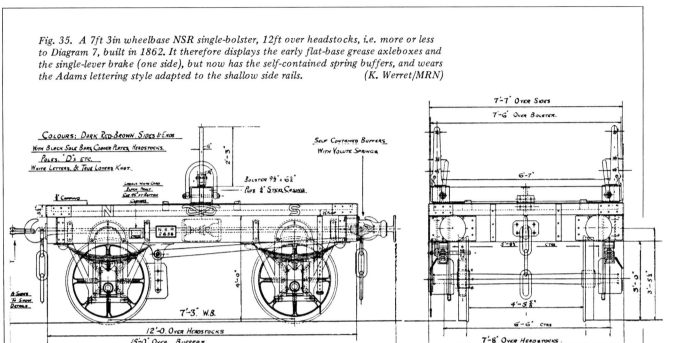

Fig. 35. A 7ft 3in wheelbase NSR single-bolster, 12ft over headstocks, i.e. more or less
to Diagram 7, built in 1862. It therefore displays the early flat-base grease axleboxes and
the single-lever brake (one side), but now has the self-contained spring buffers, and wears
the Adams lettering style adapted to the shallow side rails.　　　　(K. Werret/MRN)

Timber wagons or trucks appear to be little documented in the North Stafford records, and yet the company had 325 rail or timber wagons in 1920. The surviving NSR Wagon Diagram Book shows:

Diagram 7: A 7ft 0in wheelbase Single (swing) Bolster Timber Truck, 12ft 0in over body, 7ft 8in wide, Tare 4.19.1.

Diagram 8: Twin Timber Truck(s): 2/9ft 0in wheelbase Single Bolsters permanently joined, each 15ft 6in over body, 7ft 8in wide, Total tare 11.9.3.

Diagram 19: 15 ton Rail truck, 20ft wheelbase, 31ft over body, Tare 8.8.2.

Also, differing only in the cradles, rather than bolsters, were:

Diagram 17: Twin Boiler Trucks, dimensions as Diagram 8.

Diagram 17: 15 ton Boiler Truck, dimensions as Diagram 19.

The single bolster timber trucks to Diagram 7 – and boiler trucks very similar to them – seem to have been built over a long time, but with the usual variations in ironwork and undergear, as the following examples will show:

Boiler Trucks 3471 & 3510 – appear dimensionally as Diagram 7 except for the boiler cradles. Differences in detail are: no side rails, dumb buffers, 1870 flat base axle boxes, single lever brake one side only (with large brake blocks), tie rods between axle guards. Unpainted, but lettering centrally on solebar (pre-1912 style). 7ft wheelbase, 12ft over headstocks

Single Bolster 2658 – one of 20 built by Joseph Wright & Sons in 1862 (Nos. 2654-2673). Wheelbase given as 7ft 3in, side rails and corner plates, single lever brake one side only, flat base axle boxes, self-contained spring buffers. Number plate on solebar, lettering (post-1912) on side rail. 12ft over headstocks.

Single Bolsters 3437 & 1551 – dumb buffers, single lever brake, round based axle boxes, shallow side rails with corner plates (another pair on same view have deeper side rails). Lettering (pre-1912) on side rails with 'To carry 8 tons'. Tares 4.0.0 & 4.13.2.

Single Bolster 664 – V-hanger brakes, round based axle boxes, and seems to have the self-contained rubber buffers. Number plate on solebar, lettering (post-1912) on side rail.

Single Bolster 3816 – push rod brakes both sides, round based axle boxes, self-contained spring buffers, side rails with corner plates, number plate on solebar, post-1912 lettering on side rail. 7ft wheelbase, 12ft over headstocks.

Recorded numbers for pairs of twin timber trucks are 3467 and 36, the same number appearing on both wagons, as they were permanently coupled together. One wagon to the dimensions of a single member of the twins, but buffered at both ends, was No. 1063, tare 4.16.0. This had V-hanger brakes one side only, and normal spring buffers. It is unlikely to have been part of a twin which was split up, as the underframes of the twins were not designed for separate use, and its existence suggests that other single wagons to the same dimensions had existed, though not appearing in the Diagram Book.

Plate 52. The North Stafford seems to have been content with quite a short single bolster, timber (or rail) wagon for a long time, and a number of examples are shown here. Dumb-buffered 8-ton single bolsters Nos.3437 and 1551 (and others) are loading rails at Shelton Works, all having the round-base grease axleboxes and the single lever brake; the tare is 4.0.0. The two more distant wagons have deeper side rails than the nearer pair.

Manifold Collection

Plate 53. Single bolster No.3816 (tare 4.10.2) is thought to be 15ft 6in over headstocks on a 9ft 6in wheelbase; it has heavy duty self-contained buffers, grease axleboxes, and the push-rod lever brake both sides. No.3816 is coupled to GCR (twin) single bolsters. *HMRS*

Plate 54. A detail view of the same vehicle; has the load been 'stopped' by the displaced bolster unit? *R. J. Essery*

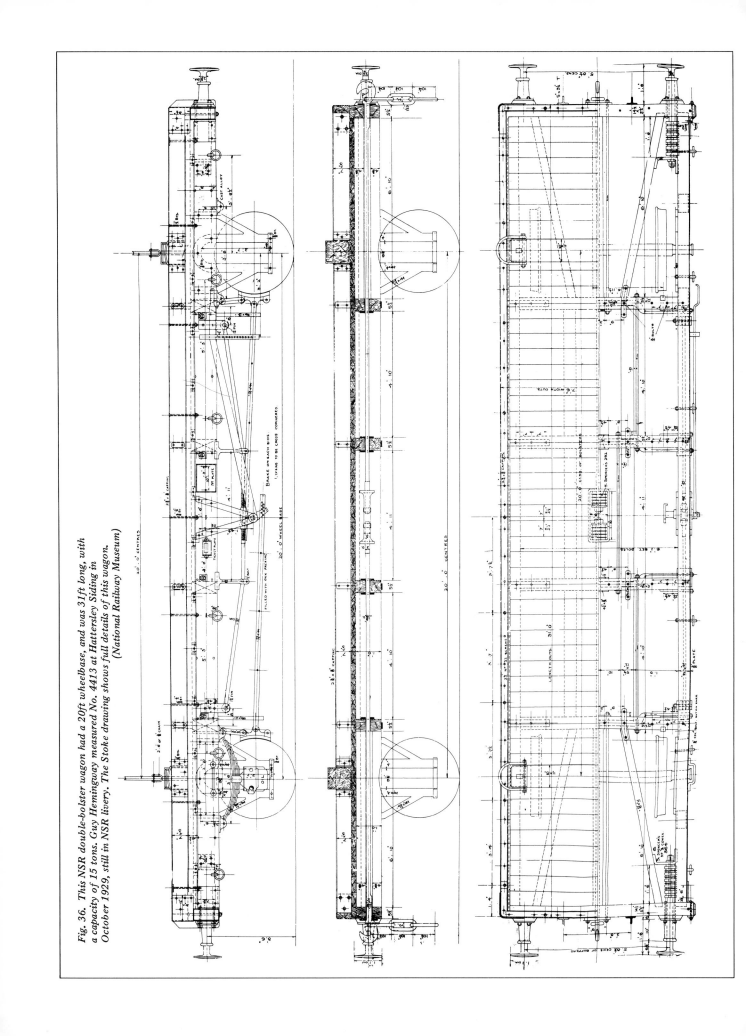

Fig. 36. This NSR double-bolster wagon had a 20ft wheelbase, and was 31ft long, with a capacity of 15 tons. Guy Hemingway measured No. 4413 at Hattersley Siding in October 1929, still in NSR livery. The Stoke drawing shows full details of this wagon. (National Railway Museum)

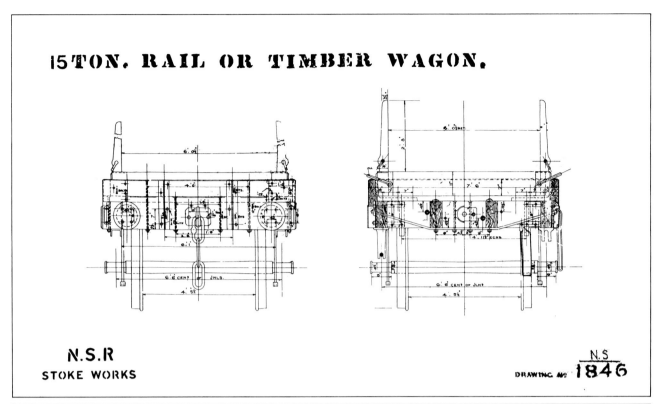

15 TON. RAIL OR TIMBER WAGON.

N.S.R
STOKE WORKS

N.S
DRAWING № 1846

Fig. 37. A 9ft wheelbase, 15ft 7in long single-bolster, measured by Guy Hemingway in NSR livery as late as June 1930; it is dimensionally similar to one of a pair of twin timber trucks to Stoke drawing No. 1937 (of 1913), Diagram 8. (Author)

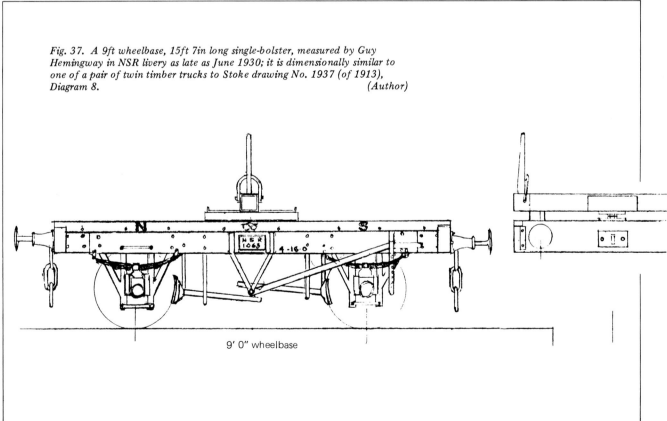

9' 0" wheelbase

Fig. 38. NSR 15-ton double-bolster wagon No. 1884, c.1914. E. G. Mackenzie

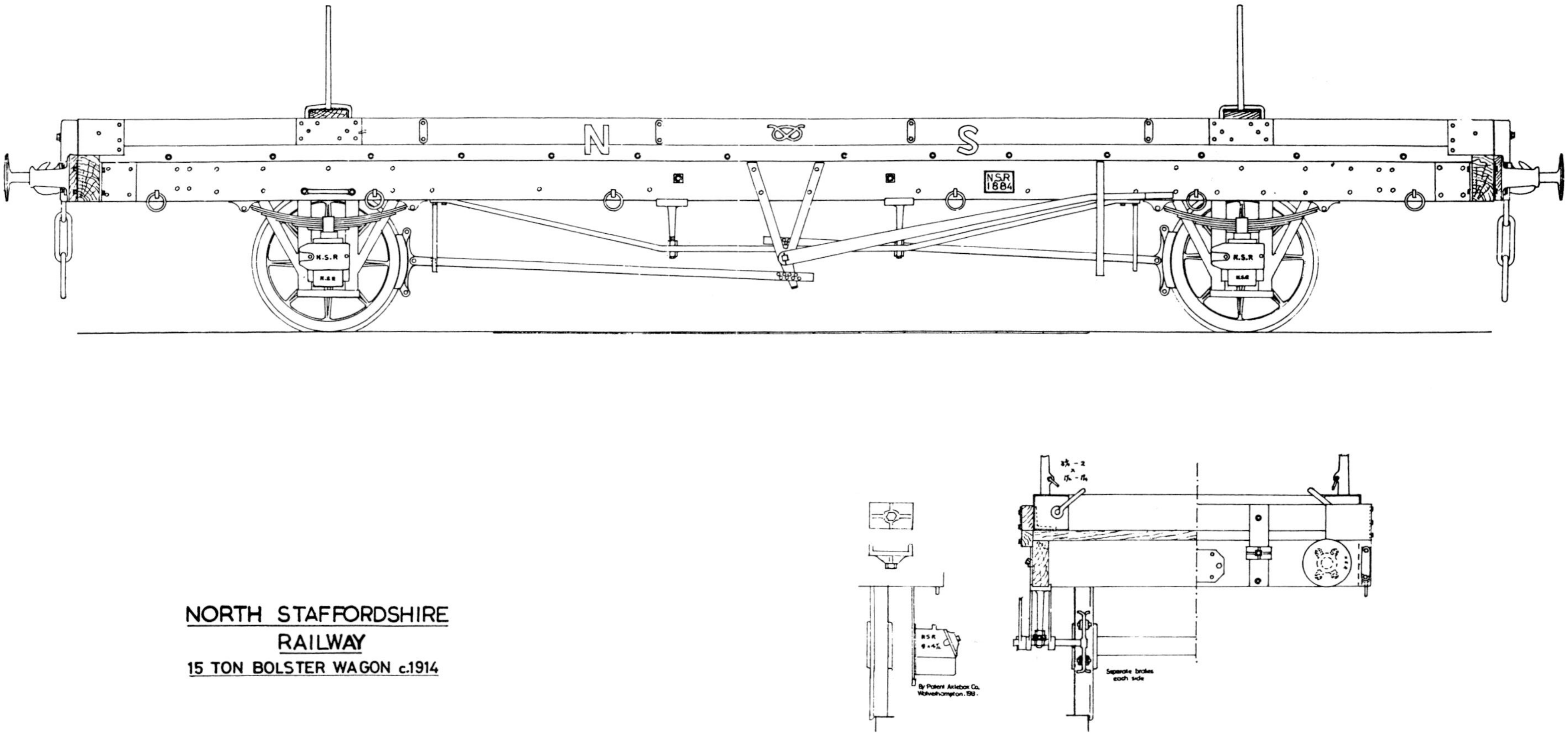

NORTH STAFFORDSHIRE RAILWAY
15 TON BOLSTER WAGON c.1914

Plate 55. Late in its life, the North Stafford acquired four of its largest and heaviest items of rolling stock, built in 1921 by the Metropolitan Company at Wednesbury. The 25-ton bogie well wagon No.4496, was one of two (tare 22.12.0), total weight on rails, loaded, 47 tons 12cwt. These were the longest as well as being the heaviest NSR wagons. *Birmingham City Libraries*

Plate 56. The Metropolitan C & W Company also supplied the NSR with two bogie rail trolleys to carry 30 tons (tare 16.10.0). One of these, No.2168, is shown in this official view. *Birmingham City Libraries*

Plate 57. Ashbourne, c.1916, with a train of J. Harrison furniture containers and a horse-drawn pantechnicon. The nearest wagon is a furniture truck to diagram 22, with drop ends, screw couplings, and vacuum pipes; it has grease axleboxes, the push-rod brake, and webbed-shank buffers. There were four such vehicles: Nos.136, 284, 308 and 640, of lengths 17ft 11in, 16ft 6in, 16ft 6in and 16ft 0in respectively, and of tare weights 5.19.3, 5.12.1, 5.7.0, and 5.11.0. The middle wagon has not been positively identified as NSR, but the furthest is a Longbottom 2-plank. The engine is 'DX' 0-6-2T No.76, an Ashbourne engine. *Manifold Collection*

Plate 58. Like all pre-Grouping railways in industrial areas, the North Stafford system was host to many private owner wagons; no attempt will be made here to give even a representative selection of such wagons, for the subject is a large one, and reference might be made to the series by Bernard Holland in *Model Railway Constructor*, 1970. Thomas Bolton & Son, No.13, was built by the Metropolitan C & W Co. at Ashbury, and had the NSR registration plate and builder's plate on the solebar; the lettering at left was: 'Thos.Bolton & Sons / Oakamoor Station / North Stafford Railway' in three lines. *HMRS*

Fig. 39. Thomas Bolton & Son, single-plank open wagon; measurements taken from No. 15, now at Foxfield Light Railway. (Author)

14' 11" over body

Buffers as NSR plain type

7' 6"

T.B&S. No.10

No.10

Axleboxes similar to NSR grease type

Brakes both sides

9' 0"

3 lines of lettering (italic)
Thos. Bolton & Sons
Oakamoor Station
North Stafford Railway

Plates 59 & 60. Thomas Bolton & Son No.15 seen at Foxfield Light Railway, showing details of ironwork (Plate 59), and the two sole-bar plates (Plate 60). Wagons Nos. 9, 10, 13 and 15 were identical; the livery was pale grey, with black ironwork and white lettering, the large letters being shaded black. *Author*

REGISTERED BY THE 1916 TO CARRY 10 TONS 11995 NORTH STAFF RY CO

ASHBURY WORKS THE METROPOLITAN CARRIAGE WAGON & FINANCE CO LTD MANCHESTER

Plate 61. Bradwell Wood (Staffordshire Chemical Company) No.123 pictured on a tippler at Milwall Docks, North London Railway, on 22nd June 1898. No.123 is fitted with a coke rave, and has brakes one side only. The other wagon also seems to be Bradwell Wood, but has a different coke rave.

National Railway Museum

*Fig. 40. Bradwell Wood 6-plank wagon No. 123, with coke rave. The
drawing assumes the wagon was built to the 1897 RCH specificiation.*
(Author)

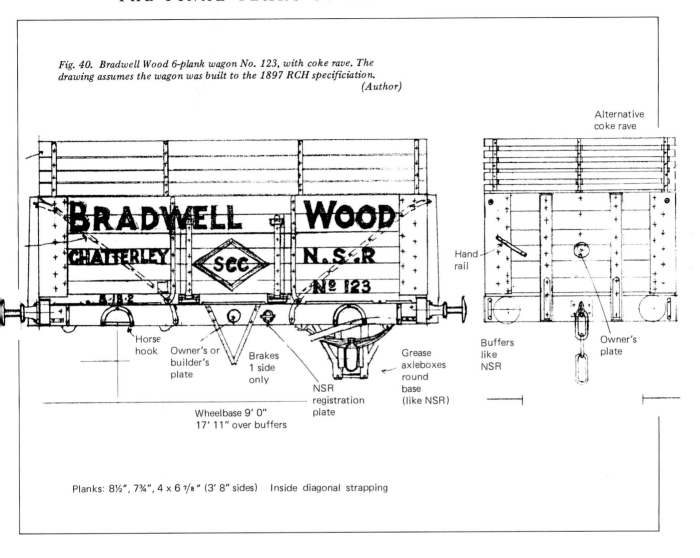

Alternative
coke rave

Hand
rail

Buffers
like
NSR

Owner's
plate

Horse
hook

Owner's or
builder's
plate

Brakes
1 side
only

NSR
registration
plate

Grease
axleboxes
round
base
(like NSR)

Wheelbase 9' 0"
17' 11" over buffers

Planks: 8½", 7¾", 4 x 6 ⅞" (3' 8" sides)   Inside diagonal strapping

Plate 62. A view of the more-or-less complete NSR breakdown train. The crane was supplied by Cowan & Sheldon Ltd. in 1895 at a cost of £1550; it was a standard design, as exemplified by two engravings in *Engineering* for 30th August 1895. The NSR crane match truck was a standard 2-plank wagon (No.4841), with V-hanger brakes one side, grease axleboxes, and webbed, (presumably heavier-duty) buffers. An old 4-compartment 4-wheel coach with end windows ran next to the match truck in Longbottom's time, being replaced by a 5-compartment 6-wheeler in Adam's version of the train. A 5-plank wagon was also included in the earlier composition, with what seems to have been a conventional goods brake van at the rear.

Manifold Collection

Plates 62a & b. When new, the NSR breakdown crane was despatched to retrieve coal wagons at Diglake which had run down an embankment. Unhappily, the crane overbalanced and itself required rescuing – a circumstance which resulted afterwards in the fitting of outriggers to the frames.   *Manifold Collection*

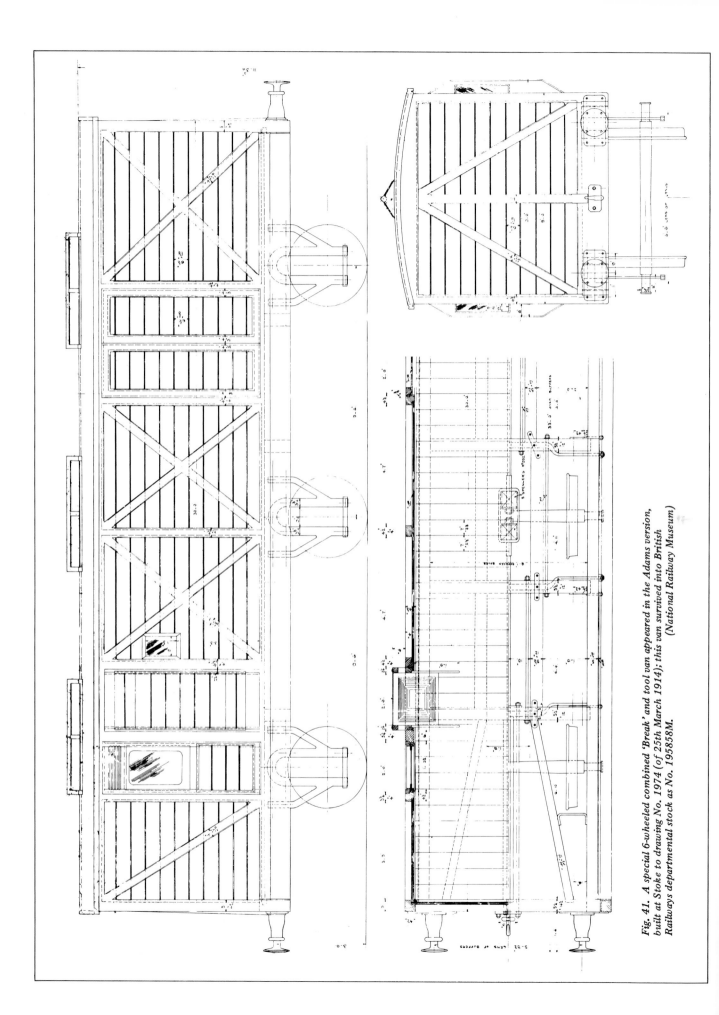

Fig. 41. A special 6-wheeled combined 'Break' and tool van appeared in the Adams version, built at Stoke to drawing No. 1974 (of 25th March 1914); this van survived into British Railways departmental stock as No. 195858M.
(National Railway Museum)

Plate 63. Another view of the breakdown train (in later form), with the 6-wheel van at the head.
Manifold Collection

Plate 64. A photograph of the NSR 6-wheel brake & tool van in later days, as DM 195848.   *J. R. Hollick*

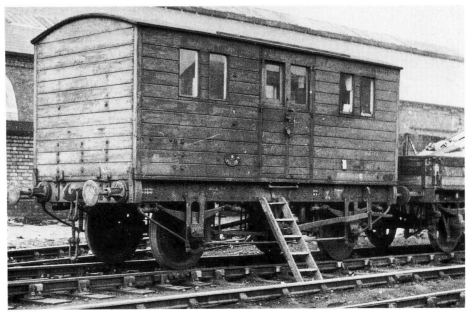

Plate 65. Another tool van, possibly for the use of other departments of the NSR, and built on an old PLV or 4-wheel coach underframe, is shown in this surviving view as LMSR No.196829.
J. Peden

Plate 66. The NSR had a number of small hand cranes used by the Engineer's Department. Two are shown here working on the widening of Bridge 84 at Scropton, with Scropton church in the background and the rails of Staton's tramway, (narrow gauge) in the foreground. The cranes are a standard design with balance weights, and were secured to the rails when operating. Locomotive-type buffers were fitted, and the vehicles were braked on one side only.

Manifold Collection

Plate 67. A similar crane, complete with men working on the hoisting gear, is seen in this view of Leek, in 1913. Alongside the crane is single bolster wagon No.664, which had V-hanger brakes and was fitted with the rubber self-contained buffers.

Manifold Collection

Plate 68.   A rake of single bolsters with a 4-wheel hand crane is seen at Trentham Park during the construction of the abortive line extension bridge in 1914.
Manifold Collection

REFERENCES

1. *North Staffordshire Railway, Contract for Locomotive Power and Carriages, 1849*, Public Record Office, RAIL 532/54.

2. *The Engineer*, 30th October 1925: 'The Evolution of the L.M.S. Railway, by Arthur Jeffkins, No. 15, the North Staffordshire Railway', in PRO, RAIL 1007/572.

3. *NSR Minute Book*, 29th June 1846 to 5th July 1851, entry for 13th January 1847, PRO, RAIL 532/4.

4. *NSR Finance Committee Minute Book*, June 1846 to August 1851, PRO, RAIL 532/10.

5. PRO, RAIL 532/70: Survey by C. F. Cheffins, Surveyor, 1846 (of various NSR branch lines); also RAIL 532/31: Contract Plans for Tunstall and Leek lines, NSR, February 1864, signed by Charles Cheffins.

6. PRO, RAIL 236/671 and /672 (4 vols.): GNR scale diagrams of goods waggons, etc., 1848 onwards.

7. The drawing of the Composite Carriage is of interest as giving a small clue to the early livery of some NSR carriages; it had the full NSR coat of arms on the first class doors.

8. D. K. Clark: *Railway Machinery*, Vol II, 1855.

9. Ibid.

10. Board of Trade: *Railway Returns for England and Wales*, HMSO, 1860.

11. PRO, RAIL 532/17, November 1861 to July 1867.

12. Board of Trade: *Railway Returns*.

13. *NSR Finance Minute Book*, September 1861 to July 1867, PRO, RAIL 532/13.

14. H. B. Holland: 'Some Birmingham Wagons', *Historical Model Railway Society Journal*, Vol. 8, p. 58.

15. Drawing No. 3856.

16. *HMRS Journal*, Vol. 8, No. 11, 1975, p. 237.

17. *Model Railway News*, August 1963.

18. L. Tavender: 'Notes on Attempts to Modernise Goods Rolling Stock', *HMRS Journal*, Vol. 5, No. 12, 1967, p. 185.

19. HMRS Gloucester Carriage & Wagon Co. Collection, No. 196.

20. *General Report to the Board of Trade upon the Accidents that have occurred on the Railways of the United Kingdom During the Year 1907*, HMSO 1908: Reports of the Inspecting Officers: Great Central Railway, Accident near Waleswood on 16th July 1907.

21. *NSR Finance Minute Book*, September 1861 to July 1867, PRO, RAIL 532/13, entry for 3rd May 1864.

22. Stoke drawing No. 167, undated.

23. July 1892.

24. Original coloured postcard in Manifold Collection.

25. Stoke drawing No. 1937, dated 28th July 1913.

26. G. F. Chadwick: 'North Staffordshire Railway Goods Brake Vans', *HMRS Journal*, Vol. 9, No. 4, 1976, pp. 88 to 91, and Vol. 9, No. 7, 1977.

27. R. Essery, D. Rowland, W. O. Steel: *British Goods Wagons from 1887 to the Present Day*, David and Charles, 1970, Chapter 7.

28. *Railway Magazine*, Vol. 8, March 1901, pp. 193 to 202.

29. Original in Shrewsbury Local Studies Library.

30. See photograph of longer 4-wheel Milk Van in an LNWR train, 1899, LGRP 21206.

31. *NSR Directors Minute Book*, No. 5, 17th September 1895 to 23rd March 1915, PRO, RAIL 532/8.

32. F. D. Tredrey: *Pioneer Pilot: The Great Smith Barry Who Taught the World How To Fly*, Peter Davies, London, 1976, p. 60.

General: 'Goods and Mineral Traffic – Part 4, The North Staffordshire Railway', by M. Waters, *HMRS Journal*, Vol. 8, No. 7, 1974, pp. 135 to 138, is a useful summary.

PRIVATE OWNER WAGONS
ON THE NORTH STAFFORDSHIRE RAILWAY

by H. B. HOLLAND

This is a listing of all firms known to have owned railway wagons, or to have operated them, tabulated by station. There are some cases where it could be argued that a different location might be more appropriate. In a few cases the same firm is listed under two locations.

The listing is the result of some 25 years research and sources are given as follows:

A indicates a name taken from non-illustrated archive material. The chief sources have been an NSR listing seen at Derby Works but now seemingly lost; records of the Birmingham Railway Carriage & Wagon Co. held at the County Record Office, Stafford; Railway Clearing House listings of 1926 and 1933; and records from wagon builders Charles Roberts and W. R. Renshaw Ltd.

A? indicates a name taken from the Truck Sales Ledger of Sneyd Collieries Ltd., but which cannot be confirmed as actually owning wagons. The ledger seems not to differentiate between loads carried in Sneyd's own or other wagons.

P indicates that photographic evidence exists. This varies from maker's photographs to partial wagons in backgrounds.

S indicates a sketch or drawing exists. Some of these are accurate drawings but the majority are sketches from Peter Matthews, A. G. Thomas, sketches made by me from photographs or entries in the Renshaw Order Book, or occasionally by other people.

I indicates a name given by people interviewed at various times but for which no other evidence has (yet) been found.

I should like to express my thanks to everyone who has helped with this project over the years. I can only urge whosoever reads this to scrutinise carefully the backgrounds of photographs as I am sure there still remain answers to queries lurking there.

MACCLESFIELD
Ashton & Holmes I. S.
Backhouse & Coppock, Bollington Mill A. 1886-92
Borough of Macclesfield Gas Dept. P.
Thomas Bayley A. 1881-2
James Brierley Ltd. I.
John Broadhead A. 1873
T. Bruffel I.
Hugh Ford A. 1871
Hall & Sons (Coal) Ltd. A. 1933. S.
Jas Hunt & Sons A. 1926
Jno Jordan & Son A? 1925
W. Ledgard & Co. A. 1926
James Nixon & Son A. 1894, 1904-7, 1926. P.
John Potts & Co Ltd. A. 1879, 1887-94, 1904-12, 1926. P. S.
J. P. Stafford A. 1926
Samuel Torr A. 1891-9
Joseph Welch A. 1926. P.
John Nicol A. 1905-9, 1926. P.
Frank Broadhurst A. 1905 both these wagons purchased by John
John Broadhurst A. 1905 Nicol but lettered as shown from new until ?

CONGLETON
D. Boulton A. 1933
John Bradbury, Bradley Green Colliery A. 1881-2
Congleton Equitable & Industrial Co-op Society A. 1926. S.
John Ford A. 1871
H. Hargreaves & Co. A. 1926
The Astbury Lime Co. Ltd. A. 1912-15

HARECASTLE/KIDSGROVE
Ball & Sons A? c.1924
Birchenwood Colliery Co. A. 1892-1900. P. S.
Daniel Boulton, Red Bull Lime Works A. 1900, 1926
Harecastle Collieries A. 1896-1900, A. 1926. S.
Harecastle & Woodshutts Colliery & Coke Co. (Bidder & Elliott) A. 1867-96
Kidsgrove Collieries A. P.
Kinnersley & Co., Clough Hall Iron Works A. 1875-86
John McGowan (Harecastle & Woodshutts Colliery) A. 1897-1900
Smallwood & Co. A. 1894
Tarmac (Kidsgrove) Ltd. A. 1926. P.
Turner & Sherwood A. 1900
Warburton & Crimes A. 1896-1900, 1926. P. S.
H. I. Williams (scrap merchants) A. 1894

CHATTERLEY
Butt Lane Co-operative Society, Talke A. 1888-91
Chatterley Iron Co. A. 1864-71. P.
Chatterley-Whitfield Collieries Ltd. A. 1900-04. P.
Goldenhill Colliery Co. P.
Goldendale Iron Co. A. 1880-84. P. S.
New Acid Co. A. 1914-26. P. S.
Staffordshire Chemical Co. (Dunn Bros) (1917) Ltd. A. 1900, 1906-7, 1926. P. (wagons lettered Bradwell Wood, c.1890) (lettered S C C 1930s)
Talk o' th' Hill Colliery Co. Ltd. A. 1887-93, 1926. P. S.
Tarbitumac P.
Wentworth Rose & Co. A. 1926

LONGPORT
Burslem Gas Works P.
John Mason A. 1888-98

ETRURIA
Bassetts Ltd. A. 1926, S. P.
Boulton & Sowter, Wolstanton A. 1875-91
Cardox Coals, Wolstanton Colliery I. P. S.
Earl Granville A. 1866-78. P.
W. Hall, Wolstanton A. 1894
Phoenix Wagon Works, Cliffe Vale A. 1894
Charles Salt, Ironstone Agent, Wolstanton A. 1891-4, 1902. P.
Shelton Iron, Steel & Coal Co. A. 1905-18, 1926. P.
G. I. Steele, Basford A. 1894
J. G. Steele, Basford A. 1894-5
Stoke-on-Trent Corporation Gas Dept. A. 1926. P. S.

STOKE-ON-TRENT
Bakewell & Butterworth Ltd A. 1926
Balmain Bros & Co. A. 1875-79
Joseph Battersby A. 1875-78
S. J. Bott A. 1891 (not certain if ran in this name)
Bott & Ecclestone A? c.1924
J. E. Cowie/Goodman & Cowie A. 1879-80
W. Craig A. 1891, 1900
John Grocock
Hale Fuels P.
J. H. Ketley A. 1896-1905. P.
John Leach P. S. I.
Potteries Coal Supply Co. P.
Charles Salt, Coal A. 1892 (Mill Hayes Colly, Burslem?)
Stafford Coal & Iron Co. Ltd. A. 1900, 1933. P.
E. Steele A. 1933. P.
J & C Waine A. 1893
John Williams & Son (Colliery Agents) Ltd. A. 1926. S.

TRENTHAM
Coking Co. Ltd. A. 1926
Florence Coal & Iron Co. Ltd. A. 1900. 1926. P.
The North Staffordshire Slag & Tarmacadam Co. Ltd. P. (the above emptied to Sideway, so perhaps should be listed under Stoke)

BARLASTON
E. Alcock A? c.1925
Buxton Bros. A? c.1924
Knight & Pointon P.
G. F. Paddock A? c.1924

STONE
John Freakley A. 1896
P. Garley A. 1894
Robert Grant A. 1906-7. S.
J. Griffiths A. 1900
Jno Griffin A? c.1924
Wm Kenderdine A. 1926
Samuel Russell A. 1900
Stone Gas & Electrcity Co. Ltd. A? 1922-25

WESTON
Earl Ferrers, Shirleywich A. 1894
Shirleywich Salt & Chemical Works A. 1894, 1900. S.

CREWE
G. Ashman A. 1925, 1933. S.
G. Astbury A? c.1925
W. J. Battams A. 1926
V. A. Bond A. 1933. P. S.
H. Chesters Ltd. A? c.1925
F. C. Collis A. 1926. S.
Crewe Co-operative Friendly Society A. 1925. P.
G. H. Dimelow & Son A. 1900-14, 1925, 1933
J. Donellan & Son A. 1906 P.
A. Edwards A. 1900
J. Gregory & Son A. 1904-13. S.
Samuel Heath Jr. P.
T. H. Heath A. 1887-89
H. Hollinshead A? c.1925
C. Hunt A? c.1925
Knowles & Cooke A. 1921-28
F. H. Lunt A? c.1924
Neville & Wilshaw A. 1905. S.
Thomas Nicholls A. 1870-71
Thomas Pepper A. 1909. S.
J. Robinson A? c.1924
F. M. Scragg A. 1900
T. & N. Scragg A. 1893-1912 (wagons may have been lettered Scragg Bros)
J. Simon & Son A. 1925-33
Slack I.
Smith & Machin A? c.1925
H. J. Williams A? c.1925
James Willshaw A. 1909-16
J. J. Wilson A? c.1925
J. N. Woodbridge A. 1933

ALSAGER
The Astbury Hydraulic Lime & Stone Co. A. 1879-1916
Joseph Boulton of Alsager and Wirksworth Dale Lime & Stone Works A. 1880-82
Joseph Brownsword A. 1926
A. E. Burgess A. 1892-3
Joseph Carr A. 1889-94
E. A. Edwards A? c.1924
J. Morris A? c.1925
Oakhanger Moss Litter Co. Ltd. A? c.1924
J. Settle P.
Settle Speakman & Co. Ltd. A. 1926. P.
J. Whitter A? c.1925

FENTON
Billy Barlow I.
Berry Hill Collieries Ltd. A. 1926. S. P.
John Challinor & Co. Ltd., Glebe Colliery A. 1887-89
Fenton Collieries Ltd. A. 1933. S. P.
Glebe Colliery P.
John Slater, Berry Hill I. P.
H. Warrington, Berry Hill Colliery A. 1907-8. S.

LONGTON
Lane End Works (Balfour & Co.) A. 1887-92. S.
Frank Lowe A? c.1924
J. Lowndes Ltd. A. 1900, 1926
Mossfield Colliery Ltd. A. 1926. P. S.
Park Hall Colliery A. 1894
Parkhouse Colliery, Adderley Green A. 1900
Rigby & Co. (Mossfield Colliery Co.) A. 1884-1917
Stirrup & Pye, Adderley Green Colliery A. 1907. P. S.

BLYTHE BRIDGE
Foxfield Colliery Co. Ltd. A. 1893, 1926. P. S.
Park Hall & Foxfield P.

CHEADLE
Bassano Bros., New Haden Colliery A. 1907-10
Cheadle Gas Works I.
Cheadle Park Colliery P.
Draycott Colliery Co. A. 1900-06
R. Plant A.

UTTOXETER
Bamfords Ltd. A. 1926
P. C. Brisbourne A. 1925
Brisbourne & Nevill A. 1926
Eckerley Bros. A. 1903-12, 1926. P. S.
N. S. R. Employees Coal Association A. 1903-06
Uttoxeter Gas Works Ltd. A. 1916, 1926

SUDBURY
William Archer, Scropton A. 1921
G. H. Bakewell, Scropton A. 1901
Charles Evans, now Thomas Henry Cook (sic) A. 1906-11
Job Jackson A. 1901, 1910, 1926

TUTBURY
Charles Clark A. 1896
Joseph England (or Hough & England) A. 1893-98
Fanny Ford (late W. G. Ford) A. 1897
William Hughes A. 1899
R. G. Roberts (later A. G. Roberts) A. 1909
Thos. Shipton A. 1894-96, 1916, 1926
J. G. Staton & Co., Shobnall Mills A. 1880-1899. P.
G. White A. 1894

RUSHTON
George Collins I. A. c.1924
James Goodfellow I.

RUDYARD
G. T. Heath A? c.1924
Mrs. B. C. Shaw A? c.1924

LEEK
R. Brindley & Son A. 1889-1914. S.
S. Brindley A? c.1924
Thomas Cheetham A. 1870
Charles Fogg A. 1904. S.
Foresters Ltd. A. 1926
James Goodwin A. 1926. S.
Henry Hall & Son A. 1900
C. S. Herd A? c.1924
T. Jepson & Co. A? c.1924
Leek U.D.C. (Gas Works) A. 1926. I.
Leek & Moorlands Co-op Society Ltd. A. 1926. P.
Leek Coal Co. A? c.1924
Henry Machin P.
H. W. Nixon A. 1894
F. Parr A? c.1925
W. Pickford & Co., Californian Mills A. c.1925
John Potts & Co. A. 1902-14
W. Scotton A? c.1925
T. A. Thursfield A? c.1925
J. Williams A? c.1924

KINGSLEY & FROGHALL
Thomas Bolton & Sons Ltd. A. 1917. P.
Bowers & Thorley A. 1894. P.

OAKAMOOR
T. Bolton & Sons Ltd. A. 1891, 1926. P.

ALTON
J. H. Hammersley A? c.1924

ROCESTER
T. B. Dyer A. 1926
C. A. Hartley (t/a The Red Hill Band Brick & Pipe Works) A. 1908
T. W. Langton A. 1933

NORBURY
E. A. Chell A. 1926
Henshaw & Sons A. 1874-80
Wm. Holland A? c.1924

ASHBOURNE
Ashbourne Gas Works I.
Joseph Coates A. 1869
J. O. Jones & Sons A. 1894, 1926. P.
Simpson Bros Ltd. A. 1903-19
Thomas Smith A. 1871-4
John Twigge A. 1887-9

NEWCASTLE
Edwin Barker & Sons A. 1901
W. J. Bates & Sons A. 1933
Farrell & Co. A. 1885-93
Jas Garrett A? c.1924
H. Goodwin & Son A? c.1924
Joseph Green, Clayton A. 1926
Newcastle-under-Lyme Corporation (Gas Works) A. 1924. S.
Orwell & Son A? 1922-24
Scragg & Mitchell A. 1900
Scragg I. (probably Samuel Scragg)
Henry Sowter A. c.1900
L. Timmis Ltd. A? c.1924
Newcastle Chemical Works Co. Ltd. A. 1874

SILVERDALE
Butterley Coal & Iron Co. A. 1900
Knutton Farm Mining Co. A.1866-97
Knutton Manor Mining Co. A. 1917. I.
John Nash Peake, Rosemary Hill Colliery, Knutton A. 1876-95
Silverdale Co. Ltd. A. 1906, 1917. P.
Stanier & Co. P.

PIPE GATE
J. Meakin & Sons I. P.

NORTON IN HALES
E. G. Keay A? 1923-27

MARKET DRAYTON
B. Allen & Son A. 1926
C. Bolton & Co. A. 1926-7
George Lee A. 1926
Market Drayton Fuel Supply Co. A. 1933. P.
J. Meakin & Sons Ltd. A. 1926. S.
S. Woodcock (later . . . & Son) A. 1900, 1926. P.

HALMEREND
Cooper & Craig P.

AUDLEY
The Audley Coal & Iron Co. Ltd. A. 1875-1904
Bignell Hill Colliery Co. Ltd. A. 1926. P.
J. H. Proctor A. 1894
William Rigby & Co., Bunkers Hill Colliery A. 1884-1904

LEYCETT
Brick & Tile Workers S.
Crewe Coal & Iron Co. A. 1867. P.
Madeley Coal & Iron Co. A. 1900. P.
Madeley Coal, Coke & Brick Co. (1905) Ltd. A. 1905-16. P.
Madeley Collieries Ltd. P.

HANLEY
James Audley, Granville Place, Cobridge A. 1878-90
Harrison & Son (Hanley) Ltd. A. 1926
Lovatt, Warrington & Co. A. 1924. P.

BURSLEM
John Brindley, Wedgwood Saw Mills A. 1882-87
Burgess & Leese, Burleigh Pottery I.
Burslem Gas Works P. (probably at Longport, q.v.)
Chaddock Myring A. 1894
Burslem Coal & Iron Co. A? c.1924
John Holdcroft A? c.1924
George Humphries A. 1876-82
Mill Hayes Mining Co. A. 1873
The Sneyd Colliery & Brickworks Co. Ltd. A. 1891-94
Sneyd Collieries Ltd. A. 1900
Wildblood Bros. A? c.1924
Josiah Patrick Wise, Stanfield Colliery A. 1879-81

TUNSTALL
Wm. Adams & Sons (Potters) Ltd. A. 1900-15, 1926
F. H. Bankart, Turnhurst Colliery A. 1870-72
Bray & Thompson, Heybridge Alum Works A. 1870-72
Edwin Butterfield, Brownhills A. 1871-72
John Butterfield as agent for the late H. H. Williamson A. 1870-72
Clive Son & Myatt, Clanway Collieries A. 1879-1900
J. Hardman & Co. A. 1884-93
Lawton Bros., Packmoor Colliery A. 1880-81
John Nash Peake, Tileries Collieries A. 1876-82
Thomas Peake, Tileries Collieries A. 1879-85
Henry Pointon & Co. A. 1905
J. Stoddard & Son A. 1926 (? — Bradley Green Colly, Biddulph)
Tunstall Coal & Iron Co. (Chell & Turnhurst) A. 1900
Turnhurst Colliery Co. A. 1874-81
Wallis & Ketley A. 1926

NEWCHAPEL & GOLDENHILL
The Wedgwood Coal & Iron Co. A. 1870-82

BUCKNALL
Hanley & Bucknall Coal Co. Ltd. A. 1870
Hanley Colliery Co. A. 1900. P. (Hanley Borough Colliery Co.)
The Ivy House & Northwood Colliery Co. Ltd. A. 1878-80

MILTON
Josiah Hardman Ltd. A. 1884-1900, 1926. P.

ENDON
Lloyd & Co. S.
Lloyd & Stacey I.

FORD GREEN
Robert Heath & Sons A. 1894. P.
Robert Heath & Low Moor P.
Norton & Biddulph Collieries Ltd. P.
Samuel Taylor & Sons A. 1897. S.

CHELL
Robert Beswick, Chell Colliery A. 1869-75
Chatterley-Whitfield Collieries Ltd. A. P.
James Edge P.
Tunstall Coal & Iron Co. Ltd. A. 1900

BLACK BULL
Robert Heath & Sons A. 1894. P.
Robert Heath & Low Moor P.
Norton & Biddulph Collieries P.

BIDDULPH
Holt Bros. A. 1926
Hurst Vale Colliery Co. A. 1875-81
Lloyd & Co. A. 1926
John Stoddard & Son A. 1908 (see also Tunstall)

CHESTERTON
Apedale Slag & Tarmacadam Co. Ltd. A. 1926. P. (lettered Slagdale)
H. Blairs A? c.1924
Chesterton Chemical Co. A. 1900 (taken over by Major & Co.)
Chesterton Colliery Co. A. 1879-80. P?
Cooper & Craig, Podmore Hall Colliery P.
William Espley & Co., Beazley Works A. 1895-97
A. D. Farrell A. 1885-87 (also at Newcastle & Tunstall)
T. W. Hall S. (this may be a misreading for W. A. Hill, q.v.)
Hem Heath Mining Co. A. 1889-92
William Hewitt A. 1892-93
John Hill, Apedale A. 1876
W. A. Hill, Apedale A. 1909, 1918, 1926. S. (lettered H A)
Holditch Mines S.
Knutton Iron & Steel Co. Ltd., Apedale A? 1924-25
Midland Coal, Coke & Iron Co. A. 1879-1900, 1926. P.
Midland Tar Distillers Ltd. (Tar Residuals Ltd.)
New Hem Heath Mining Co. A. 1926. P.
North Staffs Brick & Tile A. 1893
Parkhouse Collieries Ltd. P. S.
J. H. Pearson Ltd., Parkhouse Ironstone Mining Co. A. 1917.
Whitebarn Co. A. 1864

LAWTON
North Staffordshire Coal & Iron Co., nr. Lawton A. 1867-76
Smallwood Bros. A. 1873-76

ETTILEY HEATH
George Jepson A. 1901-03
Whitehead & Brereton A. 1873-75

SANDBACH
J. Branson & Co. A? c.1924
Edwin Foden A. 1875
Fodens Ltd. A. 1926
Jackson Bros. A. 1926. S.
Palmer Mann A. 1926. S.
J. Ruscoe A? c.1924
Sandbach Industrial Co-op Society Ltd. A. 1926. S.

LOCATIONS NOT IDENTIFIED
Dunkirk Colliery Co. A. 1866-77
F. Goddard & Sons A. 1864
Henry Hargreaves A. 1864-68
W. Hargreaves A. 1864
J. C. Harvey A. 1864
Leigh & Bradbury A. 1864
Victoria Salt Co. A. 1872-74

CRESSWELL
R. Plant A. 1877

NORTH STAFFORDSHIRE RAILWAY
ROLLING STOCK RETURNS
From Board of Trade Return, 1920

Locomotives:	Tender	53
	Tank	139
	Rail Motors	3
Carriages:	Of Uniform Class	264
	Composites	75
	Luggage, Parcel & Brake Vans	16
Carriage Trucks		24
Horse Boxes		47
Miscellaneous Coaching Vehicles		100
Wagons under 8 Tons		—
Wagons between 8 & 12 Tons		5323
Covered Wagons under 8 Tons		9
Covered Wagons between 8 & 12 Tons		336
Mineral Wagons between 8 & 12 Tons		18
Cattle Trucks		66
Rail & Timber Trucks, including Twins		325
Miscellaneous Goods Waggons		2
Brake Vans		127
Railway Service Vehicles		363

NORTH STAFFORDSHIRE RAILWAY: ROLLING STOCK FROM 1860

Source: Railway Returns for England and Wales, Board of Trade, HMSO,
latterly, 'Return No. 3, Working Expenditure, Net Receipts, and Rolling Stock'.

Year at 31st December	Locomotives	Railmotors	Carriages used for conveyance of passengers only	Other vehicles attached to passenger trains	Wagons of all kinds used for the conveyance of livestock, minerals, or general merchandise	Any other carriages or wagons not included in the preceding columns	Total number of vehicles of all descriptions for the conveyance of passengers, live stock, ballast, etc
1860	66	–	173	–	2286	–	2525
1861	66	–	174	95	2167	24	2526
1862	68	–	174	95	2289	24	2650
1863	68	–	175	119	2411	78	2851
1864	70	–	177	114	3643	3	3937
1865	76	–	177	114	3893	–	4260
1866	82	–	192	116	3893	–	4283
1867	92	–	196	117	3893	–	4298
1868	92	–	192	76	3974	–	4334
1869	93	–	196	77	3974	–	4340
1870	93	–	196	76	3974	–	4339
1871	93	–	196	76	4484	40	4889
1872	103	–	196	74	4988	48	5409
1873	103	–	199	75	4988	50	5312
1874	116	–	201	75	4988	60	5324
1875	118	–	209	75	5008	60	5352
1876	125	–	219	80	4978	60	5337
1877	125	–	236	80	4960	60	5336
1878	125	–	245	83	4961	60	5349
1879	125	–	241	87	4961	60	5349
1880	125	–	241	92	4961	60	5354
1881	125	–	239	94	4961	60	5354
1882	125	–	240	94	4962	65	5361
1883	125	–	246	94	4963	65	5368
1884	125	–	253	96	4964	65	5378
1885	127	–	256	99	4964	66	5385
1886	129	–	256	101	4964	66	5387
1887	131	–	256	103	4964	66	5389
1888	131	–	256	105	4967	66	5394
1889	131	–	256	111	4969	72	5408
1890	131	–	258	116	5080	72	5526
1891	134	–	276	117	5081	78	5552
1892	138	–	276	117	5281	78	5752
1893	142	–	276	117	5281	78	5752
1894	144	–	276	123	5281	84	5764
1895	147	–	276	130	5306	84	5796
1896	150	–	277	133	5306	84	5800
1897	152	–	275	138	5407	90	5910
1898	154	–	275	141	5511	94	6021
1899	155	–	275	141	5658	100	6174
1900	161	–	281	141	5836	106	6364
1901	163	–	281	141	5840	112	6374
1902	163	–	281	141	6095	122	6639
1903	165	–	281	142	6285	122	6830
1904	169	–	285	143	6289	122	6839
1905	169	–	287	143	6289	122	6841
1906	169	2	285	149	6289	122	6847
1907	169	2	285	149	6288	131	6855
1908	171	2	285	149	6288	132	6856
1909	173	2	285	149	6288	132	6856
1910	175	2	285	149	6288	132	6856
1911	175	2	285	149	6288	132	6856
1912	175	2	285	149	6338	132	6906

This series of Returns was interrupted by the War of 1914-18, and not resumed until 1920, in a somewhat different form (see p. 93).